A PRACTICAL GUIDE
for the
GENEALOGIST IN ENGLAND

Second Edition

By Rachael Mellen

HERITAGE BOOKS, INC.

Second Edition – revised and expanded

Published 1987 By

HERITAGE BOOKS, INC.
3602 Maureen Lane, Bowie, MD 20715

ISBN 1-55613-050-3

This book is dedicated to the memory
of my mother, Betty Butler, 1916-1984

ACKNOWLEDGEMENTS

There are so many people without whose generous assistance and encouragement this book would not have been written: primarily my husband, Robert, and children, Elizabeth and Robin. Barb Harl patiently typed the manuscript, several times, and my sister Ruth Dipple helped with snippets of research.

Many thanks go to Alan Crosby for the beautiful maps in Chapters 4 and 5, and to Mr. A. M. Wherry and Miss Jean Kennedy of the Hereford and Worcester and Norfolk Record Offices for granting permission to reproduce records in their jurisdiction. Finally, thanks go to Karen Ackermann for her thoughtful and perceptive suggestions which allowed the book to take a readable shape.

TABLE OF CONTENTS

INTRODUCTION

1980. A cool July day in a remote village in County Durham. My nephew and I spent the morning combing the parish cemetery for Bonds and Turners, ancestors of my husband, with some success on the Bond side. An inquiry in the local grocery shop sent us on a visit to the retired school teacher, the authority on local history. She happened to be living on property once owned by my husband's ancestors and she took us to the gentleman who now owned the Bond Foundry. Interesting, to be sure, but not sensational!

I decided to head for the parish church to ask about examing the burial records. It was a Saturday and a little old lady, Miss Gill, was arranging flowers for a wedding. I asked her about reading the registers and discovered that the priest was in Durham all morning, much to my disappointment. (Moral: Never ask to search registers on a Saturday.)

The lady asked me why I was interested in the parish registers; I told her I was searching for the burial of Abraham Turner. Her face lit up: "Old Abraham Turner! Why yes, when I was a little girl I saw a painting of him in his guards' uniform."

Eureka!

Miss Gill was only too eager to explain that she had regularly, as a young girl, visited Abraham Turner's widow, who was born a Bond. She remembered Mrs. Turner as a china doll lady dressed in black, with white hair and a lace cap. As we came out of the church, Miss Gill showed my nephew and me the house where Mrs. Turner had died. Miss Gill, the daughter of a foreman in the Bond foundry, filled me in on many little details of the family and local history. Even though this was only 'hearsay' evidence, it confirmed other evidence and stimulated my desire to find out more. To see and be there - that is the stuff of living family history.

Two years later, I re-visited Miss Gill with my American husband, great-great-great grandson of Mrs. Turner, so that he could hear Miss Gill's stories himself. We had tea in her drawing room overlooking the Pennines and the family returned to its origins.

Not everyone who visits England in search of their ancestry will be thus rewarded but the prospects of a rich harvest are great. With proper preparation and realistic objectives, you can locate valuable docmentary evidence, acquire a true appreciation of your ancestors' homeland, perhaps contact distant relatives, and certainly make new friends. This manual will attempt to aid you in your preparations and guide you in your searches.

CHAPTER 1

THE BASICS OF ENGLISH GENEALOGY

Genealogy is an increasingly popular hobby, particularly since the Bicentennial celebrations and the publication of *Roots* by Alex Haley. Haley's book has given encouragement to many to trace their family's history even though they may have come from a very humble background. Genealogy now has a mass appeal.

So where do you begin? How will you organize your findings? What do you need to know about English history and geography? In this chapter, I will answer these questions sequentially.

Where To Begin

Genealogical research always goes from the known to the unknown. Your first task is to collect data on yourself: weed out your birth and marriage certificates, and any diaries, letters, or journals you may have kept. Get your children's certificates, too. You are now ready to fill in a Family Group Sheet. See Fig. 1A.

The Family Group Sheet outlines three generations. It is a very important tool as it summarizes at a glance the status of your research. There are spaces for all the basic facts about one couple, including vital statistics on their parents and their children. Note the space for sources at the bottom; this will remind you where your information came from and allows you to double-check at a later time and avoid repetitious research. When you are certain your facts are correct, use ink; if in doubt, use pencil.

Branching Out

Having collected as much about yourself as possible, the next step is to interview (in person or by letter), all your older relatives. This can be difficult if the relative is in ill-health or if some family feud is still smoldering, but you will probably be surprised at how pleased many old folks are in the interest you express in their parents and grandparents.

Take along a tape-recorder if possible; you can then have a fairly natural conversation without seeming like a news-reporter. Jot down a list of questions about the subject's family beforehand, but don't feel compelled to stick religiously to the list. Rambling diversions can sometimes lead to important clues. Be aware that there may be a 'skeleton in the closet', which, even after many years, a person is still anxious to hide. Respect their right to privacy. It will make your research more challenging, but it pays to be tactful.

Sometimes the subject may not be aware of the 'skeleton': I could never garner any information from my grandmother about her father-in-law except that he died accidentally in 1911. Later research revealed he was illegitimate - a fact he probably tried to 'forget'.

Family Documents

By the time you have interviewed all possible relatives, you may have also acquired photographs, letters, diaries, certificates of birth, baptism, marriage and death, plus family bibles, passports, and other family documents. These are important in confirming the oral facts you have heard and can be divided into two categories:

a) Primary sources: written by the people involved or someone who was there. In this category come wills, letters, diaries, birth/marriage certificates, school reports, etc. These documents have greater reliability and credibility than secondary sources because they are first-hand evidence.

b) Secondary sources: written by people who were not eyewitnesses to events referred to in the documents. In this category come obituaries (which often describe events that took place before the informant's own birth), death certificates, family bible records (to some extent), oral history, and newspaper reports. These sources may not be totally reliable and must, if possible, be backed up by a primary source. It is for this reason that genealogists become so involved in searching for birth and marriage certificates and, in an earlier period, church records of baptisms, weddings, and burials.

Fig. 1A FAMILY GROUP SHEET

Name and address of researcher:

Husband's name:
Born - place & date:
Married - place & date:
Died - place & date:

Wife's name:
Born - place & date:
Died - place & date:

Husband's father:
Born - place & date:
Married - place & date:
Died - place & date:

Wife's father:
Born - place & date:
Married - place & date:
Died - place & date:

Husband's mother:
Born - place & date:
Died - place & date:

Wife's mother:
Born - place & date:
Died - place & date:

Other date about husband: religion _____ occupation _____ names of other wives _____

Children

Name	Sex	Date of birth of baptism	Place	Spouse's name & date of marriage	Date of death or burial	Place
1.						
2.						
3.						
4.						
5.						
6.						
7.						
8.						
9.						
10.						
11.						
12.						
13.						

Sources:

Fig. 1B PEDIGREE CHART

Name and address of compiler:

Chart #_____

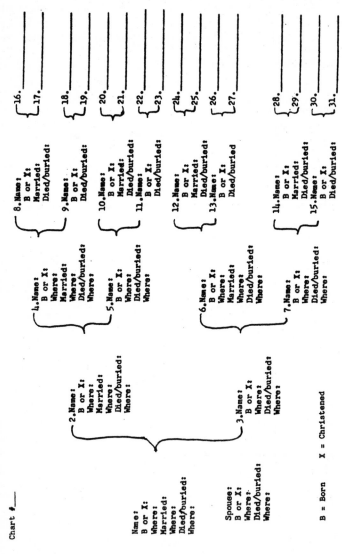

Name:
B or X:
Where:
Married:
Where:
Died/buried:
Where:

2. Name:
B or X:
Where:
Married:
Where:
Died/buried:
Where:

4. Name:
B or X:
Where:
Married:
Where:
Died/buried:
Where:

5. Name:
B or X:
Where:
Died/buried:
Where:

8. Name:
B or X:
Married:
Died/buried:

9. Name:
B or X:
Died/buried:

10. Name:
B or X:
Married:
Died/buried:

11. Name:
B or X:
Died/buried:

6. Name:
B or X:
Where:
Married:
Where:
Died/buried:
Where:

7. Name:
B or X:
Where:
Died/buried:
Where:

12. Name:
B or X:
Married:
Died/buried:

13. Name:
B or X:
Died/buried

14. Name:
B or X:
Married:
Died/buried:

15. Name:
B or X:
Died/buried:

3. Name:
B or X:
Where:
Died/buried:
Where:

Spouse:
B or X:
Where:
Died/buried:
Where:

16.
17.
18.
19.
20.
21.
22.
23.
24.
25.
26.
27.
28.
29.
30.
31.

B = Born   X = Christened

Documenting Your Findings

Now begin to build a framework of the solid evidence which you have unearthed about your family members. The Pedigree Chart is a map of the family, the sign posts being your direct ancestors. (See Figure 1B.) Begin on the left with #1 (yourself) and work across to the right, filling in as much data as you can. Use pencil if you are not sure of your facts. Names should always be written thus: John SMITH. If the person was better known by a nickname, write this in parentheses: John (Kipper) SMITH. Dates are always written with the number first, then month abbreviated in capitals, and the year in full. For example, 10 APR 1852. Pedigree charts are standard amongst genealogists. Later you may find yourself exchanging charts with hitherto unknown relatives, so make sure you follow the standard formula.

After the chart is filled in, your next step is to recheck the information on each generation by gathering the necessary birth, marriage, and death certificates. In the U.S.A., vital statistic registration is a recent innovation; in Illinois, for example, it was not compulsory until 1916. To find out when your state began registration, call the county clerk's office or write to the U.S. Government Printing Office, Superintendent of Documents, Washington DC 20402 and ask for the pamphlet, *Where to write for birth, marriage and death certificates*; this lists addresses for each state, record dates, and certificate costs.

Due to the relatively late arrival of vital statistic registration in the United States, you may find it necessary to visit and/or write to churches in the towns in which your ancestors lived. Many churches have records dating from the early nineteenth century, some go back to the eighteenth century. But beware! The records may be written in Latin, German, Polish, Italian, or French, depending on the nationality of the immigrant group which they served. NOTE: Some churches do not allow record searching. In such a case, tact and patience are the researcher's main assests, but it may be necessary to rely on diaries, probate, or guardianship records. You cannot force an institution to show its records.

Wills are an important primary source. Leaving a will has been a much more common practice in the United States than in Britain, due to the fact that more people were property-holders in the U.S. Wills and other probate documents can name a large proportion of the deceased's family and include such facts as the deceased's name, residence and date of death, list of property and heirs, testators and executors.

4

Since photostat copies are relatively inexpensive, a copy of a probate record would be a better 'buy' than a death certificate. (Death certificates usually contain the following facts: deceased's name, date and place of birth, cause and date of death, deceased's parents' names. However, these details vary between states and are likely to be less complete before the 20th century.)

One major source of secondary information is the cemetery inscription. Although the amount of information varies enormously from stone to stone, the inscription can give you some unexpected leads and it is important to find out if a tombstone exists. Copy the inscription verbatim, even apparent misspellings, and, if possible, take a photograph. (See Chapter 6). Vandalism and erosion may eliminate this source if you wait too long!

Finding Out Where Your Ancestors Came From

By now you have probably reached back to the nineteenth century or even earlier. From tombstones, letters, or oral tradition you may have a good idea whence your ancestors emigrated and when. How can you confirm this? There are three main sources:

a) Censuses, taken every ten years since 1790 (except 1940), have become more and more detailed. Before 1850, censuses listed only the head of household by name; the rest of the family and servants or slaves were categorized by sex and age, and were not named. The early censuses therefore have a more limited use, especially as country of origin was not noted. Since 1850, the censuses have shown the place of birth (usually given as a state or county); since 1880, the birthplace of parents has been given; on the 1900 and 1910 censuses immigrants had to state their year of arrival. (Unfortunately, the 1890 census was almost completely destroyed by fire.) If you do not know where your ancestors were residing in 1900 or 1910 there is a Soundex (index) on microfilm which can be consulted through interlibrary loan. Libraries can also obtain microfilm of the census this way.

b) Naturalization records were held at county courthouses until the formation of the Immigration and Naturalization Service in 1906. Prior to 1906 information obtained in records was so sketchy as to be worthless genealogically; after that date, however, much fuller statements were required. Thus, after 1906, naturalization papers gave the petitioner's name, address, last address in the country of origin, birthplace, parents' names (including mother's maiden name), port of entry into the U.S., and date of entry. Copies of declarations of intention and petitions for naturalization may be obtained by sending for form N-585 from the Immigration and Naturalization Service, 119 D Street NW, Washington DC 20536, and returning it with the appropriate fee.

c) Ships' passenger lists and customs records: provide the most complete information on the immigrant. After 1820, this included name, last residence, age, occupation, port of embarkation, and destination in the United States. Some ports have been fully indexed, 1820-1874. New York (the busiest!) is indexed only for 1820-1846 and 1883-1906. If your ancestor came between 1846 and 1883, you need to know the exact date and name of the vessel - or be prepared to search miles of microfilm! The passenger index microfilms can be consulted at branches of the National Archives, established regionally.

I was fortunate enough to find an ancestor on the New York index, so I filled out Form 81 (11-84) for a copy of the complete record from the National Archives, only to be told that the original list had been lost. A great disappointment.

Help! Where In England Did My Ancestors Come From?

Perhaps you can only establish that your family is from England, or perhaps you are more fortunate and have a particular county of origin. How can you establish which town or parish was your ancestor's birthplace? This is another situation akin to searching for a needle in a haystack, but help is at hand, thanks in most part to the Church of Jesus Christ of the Latter Day Saints (the LDS Church). They are microfilming as many parish registers of England as possible and extracting all the names onto a microfiche index known as the International Genealogical Index (IGI).

The IGI is arranged by county, than alphabetically by surname. Within surnames, events are arranged chronologically. For instance, all John Smiths in one county are listed together, the first baptism being at the top of the list, the last baptism, marriage or burial at the bottom. As the program is on-going, no county is one hundred percent completed, but information on some is very detailed. You may have to go through several counties. If the surname you are searching is unusual, the IGI can give you an indication of the geographic area in which to search, if not the exact location.

To find the LDS Library nearest you, write to the Genealogical Library, 54 E. South Temple Street, Salt Lake City, UT 84111.

Each branch library can arrange to borrow microfilm from Salt Lake City for you at a cost of $2.50 for two weeks' loan. Amongst the material available to help you locate your ancestors' parish you will find:

-Boyd's Marriage Index: arranged by county and then parish. Percival Boyd attempted to build a complete index of marriages from 1536-1837; of course, he only partially succeeded, but his work can benefit you, particularly if you are researching an unusual name.

-indexes of the births, marriages and deaths registered since 1837. These are the same ones you can consult in London (see Chapter 5), but the series is not yet complete. (You will have to get the actual certificates from London.)

-British genealogies: check if yours has already been researched; it could cut down your work enormously.

-parish registers: not all, but many.

-the British Censuses, 1841-1881. (See Chapter 5.)

You can readily see that much of your research can be done on this side of the Atlantic. What a blessing this is; it means you can use your time more fruitfully in England, consulting sources that cannot be found in the United States.

Keeping Your Records In Order

Everyone has his or her own system of filing research and it is important that you have one, too. Don't just throw your notes in a folder or box hoping one day to create order out of mayhem. Devise a plan and stick with it. Here is mine: I guarantee it works for me.

For each surname I have a large brown envelope into which go all my notes. Each book or record consulted on that name is recorded on a piece of notepaper with the surname in the upper right hand corner and the place/call number/date in the left margin. These are also recorded on a Research Index (see Figure 1C), even if the search was fruitless and the index pages are numbered. Any correspondence is also kept in order and recorded on a Correspondence Index.

Fig. 1C RESEARCH INDEX

Surname of interest: Page:
Name and address of researcher:

Record repository	Call #	Description of source	Results	File #

All family group sheets and pedigree charts are in a blue folder, in alphabetical order by head of household. Spare forms are also kept in here. This is really the master index to your complete research. You should be able to quite easily look up details of any individual and the research which led you to him.

Geography Of England

It is my common experience that few Americans know the location of any English city except London – many seem to equate London and England as one and the same! Do not let this be you!

Firstly, familiarize yourself with the counties. In 1974, the boundaries were changed – some counties ceased to exist and new ones were created (see maps). You will need to know if the counties in which you are interested were affected, because each county has a record office (archives), and it would be wasteful of time and money to go to the wrong one.

You will need a more detailed map for travel in England. A modern road atlas, such as the AA Road Atlas of Great Britain, available through the British Tourist Authority, is a good start. You may also want to acquire Frank Smith's *Genealogical Gazetteer of England* (1977), which gives information on extinct chapelries, villages, and parishes as well as thriving ones.

Planning Research Objectives In England

A research trip will be costly and probably of a relatively short duration – there will not be time to waste on wild goose chases. Therefore, the key to a successful expedition is planning.

1) Organize your completed research. Read carefully through your completed work on your English lines, with a notepad at your elbow. As you read, ideas will occur for 'solutions' to the various research 'problems': when was X born?; were Y and Z his parents?; is so, how can it be proven or disproven? For each family, construct a list of ideas to follow up. If you have a particularly sticky or dead-end problem, try to discuss it with a more experienced colleague.

2) Examine your list of ideas and determine which can be followed through in the U.S. Keep in mind the tools available at LDS branch libraries.

THE ENGLISH COUNTIES
PRIOR TO 1974

THE ENGLISH COUNTIES
SINCE 1974

3) Exhaust all possibilities. This will pare down your list to research that <u>cannot</u> be done in the US, e.g.:

-parish registers not microfilmed by the Latter Day Saints program.

-parish registers searched on microfilm which you suspect may have missing pages.

-probate records.

-civil registration.

-miscellaneous records which may be in libraries or County Record Offices. (See Chapter 4 or Public Record Office Chapter 5.)

-graveyard inscriptions.

-oral interviews.

4) Lay out your research objectives in a logical order. If you need to confirm a suspicion before embarking on a second idea, plan your itinerary accordingly. (It is not always possible to do this, in which case all potentially pertinent data at the second location will have to be noted and then left to a process of elimination by subsequent findings.)

<u>Example</u>: At St. Peter's, Totting, you find the baptism of three John Halls, any of which might be your man. List them all, plus any other Halls, in your notes. At Bingham All Souls you discover a marriage entry that lists "John Hall, labourer of Totting, married Anne Bone, spinster, of this parish" with the groom's father, Zebedee, witnessing with his mark. You can now single out the correct John from your notes at Totting.

5) Write to all the locations (churches, libraries, and record offices) which you plan to visit and make an appointment. Try to describe, as exactly as possible, the records you wish to consult. The purpose of this is two-fold: firstly, to find out if that source actually holds the records you believe it to; secondly, to warn the custodian well in advance so he can have the records ready for you. In writing to parishes, give two alternate dates and enclose two International Reply Coupons (available at all U.S. Post Offices) for reply. (See

13

sample letter below.) Names and addresses of Church of England priests can be found in *Crockford's Clerical Directory*. Most LDS branch libraries hold a copy.

Sample Letter:

1234 Washington Street
Lincoln, Ohio 12345
U.S.A.

Rev. O. B. Smith
The Rectory
Middle Snoring
Gloucestershire, GL37NX
England   1 January 1985

Dear Rev. Smith,

I am conducting research into my family's ancestry and would like an appointment to read the baptismal registers of Middle Snoring from 1752 to 1812, and the burials from 1806 to 1857. Two possible dates are July 16th and 17th, whichever is most convenient to you. I am enclosing two International Reply Coupons for your use.

Yours, etc.

Record offices only need one date option when you write for an appointment, but many have limited amounts of seating and you may need to have a table or microfilm reader reserved. In addition, the archivist may be able to suggest alternative records to consult, so a brief outline of your research goals would not come amiss. (Don't be too verbose, however, as archivists are already overburdened.) Addresses of County Record Offices can be found in Appendix A.

Send your letters air-mail. Surface mail takes six to eight weeks.

General Preparations For The Visit

Your first major decision is whether to engage a travel agent to plan and book your itinerary for you, or to do it yourself. If you have never travelled abroad before, you may feel strongly tempted to visit a travel agent, discuss your hopes and plans, and sit back, confident that your vacation is in the lap of a professional. There are, however, several considerations to be made.

Make sure that the travel agent you engage is a reputable professional. Personal recommendation by close acquaintances is probably your strongest guide, though an agent's membership in a travel agency association such as the American Society of Travel Agents, or the Association of Retail Travel Agents, is also a good plus. I hope you never experience the same frustration I had when booked on a non-existent flight to London. The travel agent had failed to relay to me a change of date, causing a 24 hour delay and the necessity of changing flights. Needless to say, I have never since engaged that particular agency!

Be aware, too, that if an agent plans and books a complete itinerary for you (as opposed to merely booking a flight), you will be charged for their professional services, including such items as cablegrams to hotels. You are paying for the agent's expertise and knowledge of the travel scene of the country you are visiting.

Additionally, most smaller European hotels, unlike large American hotel chains, do not pay travel agents a commission and, of course, do not have sales representatives in the United States. Travel agents, quite naturally, will book you into the more expensive 'name' hotels – comfortable, to be sure, but tiringly monotonous the world over. If you do not want this type of vacation, plan your own itinerary.

Self-planning will mean doing a lot of homework, especially in booking your own accommodation. Air fares can be quite a jungle, too. (Even agents cannot keep up with the daily round of gimmicks being meted out be airlines!) A self-planner can feel a sense of achievement and control of his or her time, while saving money on an agent's commission and hotel bills. The following section is therefore dedicated to the self-planner.

1) Airline Reservations. When planning the season for your vacation, bear in mind these points:

–cheapest months on scheduled carriers are October through March (except Christmas) but you are less likely to find a charter flight at that time of year.

–charter flights are usually considerably cheaper than regular or discount coach tickets. Companies will offer a discount incentive to book early, for example, before mid-April.

–regular carriers have hit back with APEX fares; seats must be purchased at least 21 days in advance and you must stay at least 7 days.

- airline coupons: You may have seen notices in the class-ified ad. sections of *The Wall Street Journal* and other na-tional newspapers advertising 'airline awards' or airline coupons' for sale at up to seventy percent off the regular first-class or economy fare. These programs are based on transfer-ral of frequent-flier awards from their original earner to you via an agency. Though not strictly illegal, airline regulations do forbid transfer of awards and frown upon the activities of these agencies. However, they are almost powerless to trace the transfers and there is definitely a growing trade in coupons. If you have no compunction about using them, you can save a great deal. Booking takes several weeks.

-standby fares are offered by the major airlines to compete with the 'no-frills' brigade. Standbys are cheaper than APEX and the voucher can be purchased in advance, but you cannot be sure of a reservation until the day of the flight. Summer season is therefore a less likely time to have standby seats left, as are Christmas and to a lesser extent Easter. To find out if there are seats available you may call the airline you have selected on their toll-free number, rather than camp out at the airport. It is really an efficient system and quite pain-less as long as your schedule has some flexibility.

2) Booking Accommodations. The prospective traveler can be dazzled by the variety of alternatives available. Go over this section carefully before deciding what you want to do.

-'name' hotels exist in Britain and can be booked through the regular reservations system here in the US. Several disadvan-tages must be mentioned, however. Firstly, to be profitable the large chain hotels are usually situated in a metropolitan area such as London, Birmingham or Glasgow; okay for the conventional tourist but not for the genealogist who wishes to investigate the wilds of Norfolk! Secondly, chain hotels are impersonal and do not reflect local color to such a degree as you might want. Thirdly, they are expensive.

-'go-as-you-please tours' are arranged by companies such as Thompson's or British Airways. You select the category of hotel you want and are supplied with vouchers good for a range of hotels up and down the country (usually British 'chains' such as Embassy or Trust House Forte). These are usually less expensive than 'name' hotels, and just as comfortable with private bath and TV in each room. Many are converted from older mansions or homes and have great charm. You are

16

unlikely to find one in an out-of-the-way spot but perhaps you might compromise a little and rent a car out, an option which will be discussed in a later section.

-private hotels and guest houses range in size from a manor house down to a terraced city dwelling. Some have private baths, many do not. Smaller guest houses are usually private homes which offer 'bed and breakfast' in the tourist season. Locally they are known as b & b's.

How can you, a foreigner, distinguish the good from the bad? Write to the regional tourist board of the area in which you are planning to stay (see Appendix C) and ask for a list of approved hotels and guesthouses (establishments which are inspected regularly and meet official guidelines). The list also grades the type of accommodation from deluxe down to good, and will give the price-range and any facilities such as a bar, TV Lounge, or baby-sitting service.

You will also find on the list an intriguing variety of places offering b & b - from farmhouses to castles. One of my most enjoyable visits was to Durham, where I had a room in the castle's keep: walls fifteen feet thick, breakfast and a gourmet evening meal in the medieval great hall and all a stone's throw from the cathedral and city center.

3) How to book accommodations in advance:

-select several places in the same area, in case your first choice is booked.

-write to the proprietor, specifying your dates, the number of people in your party, and how many rooms you will need. Enclose a deposit to the value of the first night's accommodation. This should be a cashier's check for the correct number of dollars plus three extra to cover bank conversion in England.

Summary

At least one year prior to your trip:

-check over your research to date. Plan out carefully the research that needs to be done and follow through as much as possible in the United States. An outline of the genealogical research process follows:

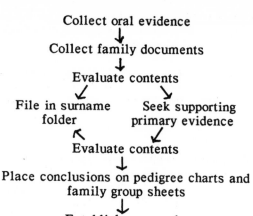

Collect oral evidence

Collect family documents

Evaluate contents

File in surname folder   Seek supporting primary evidence

Evaluate contents

Place conclusions on pedigree charts and family group sheets

Establish new goals

—make an outline of your research plans in England and plan an itinerary around this.

—write for appointments with record offices and clergy.

—write to Regional Tourists Boards for hotel lists and make reservations.

—Keep a close check on the airfare situation. Decide which type of fare best suits your needs and book accordingly.

<u>Further Reading</u>

The Genealogical Helper. Logan, Utah: Everton. (Bimonthly magazine.)

Greenwood, Val D. *The Researcher's Guide To American Genealogy*, Baltimore MD; Genealogical Publishing Co., 1973.

Smith, Frank and David Gardner. *Genealogical Research In England And Wales* (3 vols.) Salt Lake City, Utah: Bookcraft, 1959, 1964, 1976.

Westin, Jean Eddy. *Finding Your Roots* New York: Ballantine, 1977.

Wright, Norman Edgar. *Building An American Pedigree: A Study In Genealogy* Provo, Utah; Brigham Young University Press, 1974.

CHAPTER 2

WHAT TO TAKE TO ENGLAND

This chapter is designed as a checklist for the reader's convenience. Samples of charts and forms may be copied.

Genealogical Supplies

Pedigree charts
Family group sheets
Research index forms
Will forms
Census forms, 1841-1881 (Chart 1)
Birth, marriage, death registration search forms (Chart 2)
Marriage registration search records (Chart 3)
Baptismal register - search records (Chart 4)
Records of previous relevant research
An adjustable focus 35mm camera
Black and white film (print or transparency)
Colour film
Pencils with erasers
Pencil sharpener
Legal pads

Clothing & Accessories

All year round

Sturdy walking shoes
Light plastic foldaway raincoat
Light jackets or cardigans
Old jeans
Old shirt or sweater
Knee-high rainboots or slipovers
Umbrella

Winter

Heavy coat (waterproof)
Warm or thermal underwear
Gloves
Scarf
Woolly hat
Heavy wool sweaters
Heavyweight pants
Snow-type boots

Spring and Autumn

Lighter sweaters
Gloves
Headscarf or cap
Light raincoat
Shoes

Summer

Dresses
Cotton skirts
Short-sleeved blouses/shirts
Light-weight pants
Sandals
Shoes

Personal Items

Passport
International Driver's License (available from American
    Automobile Association)
Britrail pass issued by British Rail (see Chapter 3)
Coach Pass
Credit cards: Visa, Mastercard, American Express, Diner's
    Club
Travelers checks in pounds sterling
Maps: road map, small scale maps
Itinerary
List of addresses of accommodations
List of appointments booked, with addresses
Flight tickets

Note About Maps

Good road maps of Great Britain are available in most book-stores at a reasonable price, but they do tend to become out-dated extremely quickly. For the genealogist, small-scale maps of areas of interest (Ordnance Survey Maps) are available from Her Majesty's Stationary Office, 49 High Holborn, London WC1V 6HB. These maps show small details such as farmhouses and trails.

Chart 1 18__ CENSUS FOR ENGLAND

Parish or township _____   Ecclesiastical district _____

City/Borough _____   Town/Village _____

Number	Address	Name & Surname	Relationship to head of household*	Condition*	Age# M	Age# F	Rank, Profession or Occupation	Place of birth

*not included on 1841 Census
#rounded to nearest five years in 1841

Chart 2

10-YEAR BIRTH/MARRIAGE/DEATH RECORD SEARCH FORM

(circle appropriate record)

Name and address of researcher:
Date of research:

Name being researched:
Date of event (if known):

Instructions: Check space if quarter searched unsuccessfully. Fill in details of
district, and volume and page number of any possibilities.

Year	First Quarter	Second Quarter	Third Quarter	Fourth Quarter

Chart 3 MARRIAGES - RECORD OF SEARCHES

Name(s) being researched:
Date of search:
Parish searched:
Date of registers searched:
Name & address of researcher:

Date	Groom's name & status	Age	Bride's name & status	Age	Groom's parent(s) or witness	Bride's parent(s) or witness

Chart 4 BAPTISMAL REGISTERS - SEARCH RECORD

Surname(s) searched:
Parish searched:
Dates searched:
Name & address of researcher:
Date of search:

Candidates's name	Parent(s)	Date of baptism	Remarks

CHAPTER 3

COPING IN ENGLAND

Flights to England from the U.S. are at least five hours duration and can be as many as twelve from the West Coast. They are usually overnight, so it is advisable to sleep enroute to avoid the worst excesses of jet-lag. Eat a good meal beforehand and settle down as soon as you are air bound, asking the stewardess not to disturb you. Avoid alcoholic beverages. After a good sleep, drink juice or milk, eat breakfast, and exercise your limbs.

Most flights to London land at Heathrow, west of the capital, or at Gatwick, to the south. As soon as the descent begins, notice the rich green and yellow tapestry of fields interlaced, perhaps, with the silver ribbon of a narrow river; houses will seem squashed together. Britain is a tiny island compared to North America and space is highly prized, yet this also means that no-where is far away. A train trip from London to York takes less than four hours. Birmingham to London is only one hour by commuter plane, 1 1/2 hours by train.

At the airport, go first through immigration control (which means very long lines for foreigners); then, after collecting you luggage, negotiate customs control. Britain has instituted a two-channel system. If you have nothing to declare, go through the green channel. Only spot-checks are made here. If you do have duty to pay, go to the red channel. Officers will be waiting to tell you how much you owe. Having charted the appropriate course through customs, you will now push your trolley of luggage into Britain.

Private Transport

Through your travel-agent in the U.S., you may arrange to hire a car for the period, or part of the period you are in England. This option gives the traveler freedom from

27

timetables, freedom to roam at will in rural areas, freedom from such annoyances as strikes.

Both Hertz and Budget Rent-a-Car offer a weekly winter rental of about $130 for a two-door standard shift, economy-size car such as the Ford Fiesta. Such a car would be adequate for two or three adults and their luggage, and would be economical in terms of petrol (gasoline), which costs about three times the American price. There are also numerous local firms which may be able to offer a competitive price, and airlines offer fly-drive holidays, which give you a break on the cost of car-hire. The leading British car rental firm is Godfrey Davis.

When you book your vehicle, make sure that the total cost is quoted to you, including the Collision Damage Waiver, insurance and drop-off charges. Car-hire firms have a sorry history of hidden costs. !t is wise to purchase the Collision Damage Waiver (about $8 per day) to relieve yourself from worry over theft or accidents .

You will need a credit card for payment (in advance) otherwise you may have to leave a substantial cash deposit! Have your reservation number handy in case of mix-ups in the booking.

Most European cars have stick shifts, so if you must have an automatic, specify it and expect to pay extra. When you return your car, stop off at a service station and fill up the tank, or you will be charged top price for that.

Some points to remember when driving in England:

–drive on the left.

–speed limits are higher than in the U.S. and the flow of traffic, even in towns, is more hectic.

–motorways have the designation M-; for example, the M1 runs from London northwards. These roads are equivalent to American expressways. (Speed limit: 70mph)

–a roundabout is used at crossroads very often. Be prepared to halt at the edge and merge into a gap in the traffic. Signal left one exit before your intended exit. Roundabouts are not difficult to negotiate after you have tried a few.

–you may never turn right on a red light as is the case in some U.S. states.

-after a red light, you will see a red and amber combination before green appears. This tells you to prepare to go.

-all road signs are now European and mostly self-explanatory. A full list is given in *The Highway Code*, an inexpensive booklet available from Her Majesty's Stationery Office.

-front seat passengers <u>must</u> use seat belts.

-children may <u>not</u> be seated in the front of a car.
-there are stiff penalties for speeding and driving under the influence of alcohol.

It does take some guts and determination for the foreigner to venture on Britain's roads!

Public Transport

Public transport is alive and well in Britain. The national railway network (British Rail) is very extensive and buses serve even remote areas at least once a week.

Britrail Rail passes for seven, fourteen, twenty-one, and twenty-eight days may be purchased in the U.S. through a travel agent. The pass is activated by being stamped at a ticket office on its first day of use, and can be used to go anywhere in Britain within the specified period. It is a bargain when compared to purchasing separate tickets for each journey.

British Rail uses the twenty-four-hour clock in its timetables, as do bus companies. Trains are fast, comfortable and generally reliable, though the food is a national joke. Porters are available at all stations and should be tipped. All but very small stations have a buffet bar and waiting rooms.

The roadway rival to British Rail is the National Express Coach company. They run services to places often unserved by rail. A coach (the American bus), seats about 50 people and is very comfortable; a few have lavatories in the rear and some have TV's and hostesses. The major advantages are cheapness and broad scope of destinations. The disadvantages are longer journeys and poor organization at coach stations, especially Victoria in London. There is a tourist pass scheme similar to British Rail's, but it is much cheaper and does not have to be used on consecutive days; i.e. you can use up a seven-day pass over a calendar month. This represents an advantage to the traveler who wants to stay several days at various points.

Bus companies provide local, short-distance service in cities, towns, and country areas. You may have to pay the driver as you enter or a conductor will come and collect fares. State your destination clearly. Busses are often not dependable so be patient.

The London Underground deserves a section to itself. London is the only city in Britain with a subway system, but it is very extensive and for the first-time tourist, the most efficient mode of transport. There are nine lines or routes, covering much of metropolitan London. The Victoria and Jubilee lines, the most modern, are also the most clean and efficient. Some of the older lines, particularly the Northern, are dark and dirty, but travel is pleasant and safe from vandals. Beware of pickpockets, however - some things haven't changed since Dickens's time! Buy a ticket for your destination (you can choose your own route as long as you do not leave through a station). There are rows of ticket machines at most stations, but you need the correct change for these. Ticket offices are also open, if you do not have correct change.

Eating Out

In Britain eating out is not a pastime as it is in the U.S. and amongst families is usually reserved for very special occasions. You will not find the formidable array of fast-food places in every nook and cranny. Yes, McDonald's has infiltrated the conurbations but Britain has fare of its own to offer the discriminating visitor. I will survey the main types of eatery, from inexpensive upwards.

1) Fish and chips shops are open lunch times and evenings. Watch for the sign "frying times" on the door or window. Fish and chips (roughly equivalent but far superior to french fries) are no longer the cheap meal they once were, but still a great British favorite, and quite reasonable. The shop-girl will surely mutter, "Salt or vinegar?" so be prepared to answer yes or no, according to whether you want your chips doused or not. Other types of food such as cornish pasties, meat pies, and peas may also be available.

2) Cafes are friendly, homelike places, offering tea, coffee, plain meals, and desserts at a very reasonable price. They are often family run, but can be found in department stores where they are called cafeterias and are self-service. Cafes in bus or coach stations are not recommended, often being

dirty and the food inedible.

3) Pubs are open only at lunch-times and evenings, but pub fare has an excellent reputation. The menu is usually limited to cold sandwiches, pasties, pies, or shrimp or chicken 'in a basket'; i.e. with chips. At lunch-time the Ploughman's Lunch is a must: home-made bread, fresh cheese, pickled onions, washed down with a half-pint of ale. Many pubs are in historic inns and a convivial atmosphere is almost guaranteed.

4) Restaurants are much the same as in the U.S., though a town may have only one or two. Traveler's checks and credit cards are accepted. Do not expect a salad with dinner. Dishes are not described on menus but you may ask the waiter about ingredients. Some food terms are included in Appendix E.

Manners and Customs

Much emphasis is placed upon common courtesies in England - liberal use of "please" and "thank you" is much appreciated. Queuing (lining up with infinite patience) is the national pastime at bus stops, railway stations, shops, theatres - in fact, anywhere two or more are gathered. Queue-jumping must never be practiced.

Tea drinking is not merely a way of slaking one's thirst, it is the social communion of England. If you are asked to join someone for a cup of tea, try, if at all possible, to accept the offer. Britons take milk (not cream) and possibly sugar and you will be asked your preferences.

The British policeman, or 'bobby', the national symbol of integrity and helpfulness, can still be seen on foot-patrol. He is usually very good at directions, and is addressed as 'constable' (unless three stripes indicate he is a sergeant).

Many terms used in Britain will be alien even to addicts of "Masterpiece Theater". Turn to Appendix E for an English/American vocabulary list.

Climate

England is predominantly a cool, damp country, hence the ubiquitous umbrella. Showers, even heavy ones, are frequent. 'Sunny periods' and 'periods of rain' are the British meteorologists' favorite phrases.

Winters bring some fog in low-lying areas near water, but

do not expect the pea-soupers of Victorian London. Frost is more common than snow except in the North, and temperatures rarely fall below 28 degrees Fahrenheit. A cold piercing rain is common, often with high winds.

Summers are pleasantly warm, around 65-70 degrees Fahrenheit, with rain showers, and there is no need for air-conditioning. Sightseeing is enjoyable.

Spring and autumn are unpredictable seasons; it is very hard to know what to expect. Probably it is best to be prepared for the worst! Remember Keats wrote of autumn as "season of mists and mellow fruitfulness".

Electrical Gadgets

Britain's electricity supply runs on 220 volts, double that of the U.S., so any electrical appliances you take to England will require an adapter. It may be more worthwhile to use disposable razors and see a hairdresser once a week.

Currency

The units of currency are one hundred pennies (p) to one pound (£). Coins are 1p, 2p, 5p, 10p, 20p, 50p, & £1. Notes (bills) are £5, £10, £20. £1 coins are extremely unpopular and easily confused with the 10p coin. Visa is widely accepted, followed by American Express. Mastercard and Diner's Club are less well-known.

Telephones

The telephone system is a nationwide company. When dialing an in-town call, it is not necessary to dial the town code. Out-of- town calls will require the town code. International calls can be dialed direct anywhere in Britain and require use of the country code.

CHAPTER 4

RECORD OFFICES AND LIBRARIES

County councils were created by an Act of Parliament in 1889 and very soon afterwards, several councils began to take an active interest in the ancient documents within their jurisdiction. Bedfordshire created the first county office in the 1920's and has been followed by all other counties and major cities. Many incorporate the Diocesan Record Office.

Facilities for the researcher vary enormously. The number of staff can range from two to twenty, including professional archivists as well as technical and clerical staff. Space is often severely limited.

The Jurisdiction Of Record Offices

Each county or city record office varies greatly in its accessions and so it is essential to write beforehand with any specific queries you may have. Many offices have produced leaflets to help the genealogist understand the nature of their collection and what records they hold that can be of use. Below is a summary of the main types of record you may expect to find in a C.R.O.

1) Quarter Sessions Rolls. These are the documents produced by the Justices of the Peace (magistrates) in 'Quarter Sessions', that is, a quarterly convening of the county court. Most of the cases that came before the court involved only minor offenses, such as running an unlicensed alehouse, failure to repair a road or bridge, cases involving the poor and, in later centuries, non-Conformists and Catholics. Many counties have printed calendars (indexes) of the Quarter Sessions Rolls, which often date from the early medieval period.

2) Documents deposited with the Clerk of the Peace. The Clerk of the Peace was the clerk of the Quarter Sessions, and

apart from his role as a recorder, he became guardian of various types of records. For the genealogist the most important were:

–sacrament certificates (1673-1750), which prospective officeholders had to produce to prove they were communicating members of the Church of England.

–a register of the estates of Catholics, describing their properties (from 1716).

–hearth tax assessments, 1662-1688. Every householder and the number of hearths he possessed was listed for tax purposes, and some copies kept by the Clerk of the Peace have survived.

–land-tax assessments: these were the basis for the electoral roll when the franchise was based on property-ownership, and so they exist from the mid-18th century to 1832. For each property the owner's name is given, plus that of the occupier and rent paid.

–freeholders' (or jurors') lists: men aged 21-70 in each parish who qualified to serve on a jury were noted, which meant those of gentry status. In general, only about four persons from each parish are mentioned, but some counties have lists from as early as 1696.

–poll-books (late 17th century on) list names of electors.

–registers of electors (1832 on): the Parliamentary Reform Act of 1832 widened the basis of the franchise considerably and it was extended again in 1867 and 1884. From 1832 registers of electors were printed and displayed publicly. Each entry in the register gives the voter's name, address, and the nature of their qualification, for example, amount of property owned.

3) Boards of Guardians (1834-1930). By the Poor Law Act of 1834, parishes were grouped into "unions", each of which appointed a board of Guardians of the Poor to administer the Union Workhouse, which Dickens made notorious in "Oliver Twist". The Board was required to keep registers of the poor for whom they cared, as well as minute books of their meetings, in which they discussed specific cases. You may be lucky enough to find that an index has been prepared to these.

4) Censuses. The earliest censuses, 1801-1831, were the responsibility of the parish, and although they were supposed to have been destroyed, some survive and have found their way to the C.R.O. In these early censuses, only heads of household are mentioned by name. Most C.R.O.'s hold microfilm copies of the censuses 1841 to 1881 for their county. (The originals are in the Public Record Office in London).

5) Manorial court rolls. The manor court regulated village life in the middle ages. It settled minor claims and was constantly called upon to reinterpret the ancient customs of the manor and the rights and obligations of the tenants. Bromsgrove (Worcestershire) court rolls date from 1335 and its Court Leet still meets annually on the feast of St. John the Baptist, on a ceremonial basis, to weigh locally-produced bread and taste ale. The manor court dealt typically with vagrancy, non-payment of levies or dues, infringements of the rights of others (such as wood-gathering), or failure to perform a feudal duty. The court rolls teem with details of village life. Manorial rolls were usually written on pieces of vellum stitched together and rolled up. The writing is difficult to decipher, being in a cursive court hand, and is in Latin. However, printed editions of the rolls may be available, so check for these.

6) Parish records and Bishops' Transcripts (BT's). Parish records are more fully discussed in Chapter 6. It will, however, be noted that the trend towards depositing them in county record offices is increasing. This is not only extremely convenient for the researcher, but also comforting to know that these precious heirlooms from our ancestors are being carefully preserved for future generations.

Bishops' Transcripts, familiarly known as BT's, were begun in 1597, when an injunction was sent to all parishes requiring the priest to send an annual transcript of all the entries in his parish registers to the Bishop. Some priests were not very punctillious about this duty and some BT's have not survived the ravages of the centuries, but the remaining transcripts may be able to cover a gap in the original registers that is now missing or illegible. Occasionally, the transcripts may give facts in addition to those stated in the parish register or they may give a variant spelling of a surname.

7) Wills. Wills of most people of the rank of gentry or above

before 1858 are to be found in the Public Record Office at Kew (see Chapters 4 and 5), or at the Borthwick Institute in York, in the case of the northern counties. However, if the deceased did not own a substantial amount of property, the will was proved in local bishop's court, or the archdeacon's court. In this case it will now be in the diocesan record office - which often is the county record office.

The C.R.O. may have two copies of each will: the original document signed by the dying person (which are kept in annual bundles), and the full transcript entered in the court register. The will's reference number will then be identified by the surname of the first testator in the volume and the folio number - for example, Dunthorne, 162 would mean the volume beginning with the name Dunthorne, folio 162.

In many cases, a detailed inventory, or list, of the "goods, chattels and cattle" of the deceased had be added during the probate process. Usually, a small group of respectable neighbors would visit the dead person's house and write down a list of the contents, room by room, with their estimate of the value of each item or group of items appended. Many inventories give meticulous details, even to the number of sheets, chamber pots, spoons and other items modern people would consider too trivial to mention. These inventories will not further your ancestral lines, but they will provide a fascinating look into the standard of living enjoyed then and the everyday activities of your forebears.

8) Marriage allegations and bonds. When couples from different parishes wished to marry, or if they wanted to marry in a third parish, or without banns, then they had to apply for a marriage license. This meant they could furnish the diocesan office either with a BOND or an ALLEGATION. Either of these documents gave details of the couple's abode, age and occupation and the names of two sureties, one of whom was usually a parent or relative of the bridegroom. In return, they were issued with a license to marry - that is, permission.

BONDS begin with the words "Know all Men by these Present that We (the two sureties)" and involved a sum of money to be posted, although this seems rarely to have been handed over. ALLEGATIONS begin with a date and "on which day appeared personally (the groom)". Both are kept in annual bundles, but many have been indexed by ardent genealogists and local historians.

Do remember that the existence of a bond or allegation is not evidence that the marriage took place, merely an indication of where and approximately when it might have happened.

9) Non-conformist and Roman Catholic records. From 1559, when the Act of Uniformity was passed, down to the early nineteenth century, it was often dangerous and costly to be a recusant – a member of a church other than the established Church of England. This group includes Baptists, Quakers and Roman Catholics. Prosecutions for recusancy can be found in the Quarter Sessions Rolls, and as already mentioned, a register of Catholic properties was kept later on.

Quakers kept "suffering books", describing the persecution endured by its members, and also issued testimonials for members moving to another county or country (often Pennsylvania). Some of these records have been deposited in C.R.O.'s.

Most Roman Catholic registers remain in the hands of the parish priests except for Lancashire, but records of the Congregationalists, Baptists, Methodists and the Society of Friends are gradually finding their way into the record offices to be preserved.

10) Estate records. This category includes documents pertaining to private estates and although there may not be much of direct use in tracing a lineage, there are items which illustrate and add depth to the family history. Estate maps show all the field boundaries, field names (yes, every field was identified separately!), their acreages, all cottages and houses, and the names of the different owners. Enclosure maps are common from the mid-eighteenth century, when landowners consolidated their holdings and took away common land rights. They are large-scale maps, easily legible, clearly showing the pattern of land-ownership of the area.

Title-deeds to land may be preserved, but these need perseverance to be interpreted. Farm and household accounts may also be preserved and can serve as an extensive illustration of the history of an estate. F. G. Emmison in his book, *Archives and Local History*, gives the example of Audley End, Essex, for which almost 40,000 bills and vouchers exist for the period 1765-1832, all neatly sorted into categories and monthly bundles. In many cases, just a simple account ledger survives.

11) Family archives: letters and diaries. Many older families have turned over their collections of letters, papers and diaries to their C.R.O. for archival storage. The Worcester C.R.O., for example, holds letters of the Pakenhams, Russells, Devereaux, Talbots and Washingtons. There is often so much material of this type that the simple entry in the office's guide can give no indication of the richness of the find. For the researcher, this means a long process of reading and sorting, bearing in mind the problems in reading the hand of 17th century and earlier writers.

12) Printed and pictorial records. Besides manuscript and other documents, C.R.O.'s house a large variety of printed materials - photographs, picture postcards, town directories, and so on. There may also be a collection of the first Ordnance Survey of the county, about 1820.

13) School records. The beginning of public education in England lay with two charitable societies, which, in the early nineteenth century, founded many "British Schools" and "National Schools", the latter generally linked to an Anglican church. Later in the century, state education was built onto these foundations. For instance, the National School in Bromsgrove, Worcestershire, later became the Church of England Primary School, part of the state system. Log-books kept by the head-teacher contain references to the pupils (and their antics!) and registers of attendance were maintained on a daily basis. Registers might be useful in establishing an ancestor's age and residence.

Libraries

Local libraries may be an unexpected source of information. Many have acquired microfilm copies of the censuses for their area and may have a good collection of local newspapers. Most will have the Victoria County History and possibly other local histories, genealogies, and maps. A list of larger libraries with major collections is incorporated into Appendix A, but it was not feasible to include all libraries. Do be aware of their potential, however.

The Public Record Office

Ruskin Avenue
Richmond, Surrey TW9 4DV
Telephone: 01 876 3444

Open 9:30 a.m. - 5:00 p.m., Monday through Friday. Closed the first two weeks of October.

The Public Record Office has three repositories at present: Kew, Chancery Lane, and Portugal Street, London. Kew is by far the most valuable for genealogists in the variety of sources it offers for research, but the first-time visitor cannot expect to tap the P.R.O.'s resources to the full. It takes many visits and much experience to gain the most from each visit. That said, do not be discouraged - do your homework beforehand, come prepared with specific research objectives, but be flexible so you can follow up on new clues.

To consult public records you must obtain a reader's ticket in advance by writing to the above address. There is no charge for the ticket. When writing, take the opportunity to double-check that the records you wish to consult are at Kew; re-organizations do take place from time to time and you do not want to find yourself twenty-five miles from the correct repository! (Travel across London can be painfully slow and waste precious hours.)

Many of the records come from governmental agencies, such as the War Office, the Admiralty, the Foreign Office, and the Treasury. The records remain classified according to their department of origin and abbreviations are used. Some of the main abbreviations you will meet are:

ADM - Admiralty
BT - Board of Trade
CO - Colonial Office
E   - Exchequer
FO - Foreign Office
HO - Home Office
PC - Privy Council
T   - Treasury
WO - War Office
SP - State Paper Office
PMG - Paymaster General's Office
RG - General Register Office

For example, a naval record might be designated ADM 100, an army record WO 312.

. Following are the main types of records in the P.R.O.:

a) Nonconformist (or non-parochial) church registers. The P.R.O. has about 9,000 registers from churches other than the established Anglican church. They are mainly Protestant and only a few predate the eighteenth century. Early eighteenth century registers recorded baptisms, marriages and burials, but after 1754 all marriages had to be solemnized in the Church of England, and so will not show in the nonconformist registers.

There are also a few Roman Catholic registers in the P.R.O., mainly from the northern counties of England. In general, registers remain with the priest or diocese. If you have difficulty in locating a particular Catholic parish register, write to the Catholic Central Library, 41 Francis Street, London SW1P 1DN; or to the Catholic Record Society, c/o Miss R Rendal, Flat 5, Lennox Gardens, London SW1X 0BQ.

b) Wills prior to 1858. Before 1858 the proving or 'probate' of wills was purely an ecclesiastical matter and occurred in the Prerogative Court of the Province (York of Canterbury), or in the diocesan court. The P.R.O. has wills proved in the Prerogative Court of Canterbury (abbreviated to P.C.C.) from 1384 to 1858. Don't get too excited though – these are wills of persons of substantial means and the chances that your ancestor was such a person are very slim. If the surname you are researching is uncommon, however, it would certainly be worth searching the indexes described below. You may also hold the conviction that your ancestor was a notable and this is a way to document that idea.

Indexes To Wills:

-Camp, A.J. *P.C.C. Will Index, 1750-1800*. Volume 1: Surnames A-Bh, Volume 2: Surnames Bi-Ce. Completion of this project will obviously take many decades, but it is sorely needed to update the project of the British Record Society.

-*Prerogative Court of Canterbury Wills* (British Record Society). Twelve volumes spanning 1384 to 1700. Each volume covers the wills for a specific period and indexes the deceased's names alphabetically. Many large libraries and genealogical collections hold this set.

-*Card Index to P.C.C. Wills, 1721-25*: held by the Society of Genealogists.

When using these indexes, be careful to copy the full name of the deceased, date of death or probate, and reference number of the will.

Reading wills is not an easy task, especially those prior to the nineteenth century. See Chapter 9 for guidance in reading and interpreting these documents.

c) Tax records. Ever since Julius Caesar stood on England's shore and uttered the famous dictum "Veni, vidi, vici", the English people have been subjected to an ever-increasing tide of taxation. Fortunately for the genealogist, this means that lists have been generated for residents who might otherwise have gone unrecorded.

The Hearth Tax, imposed between 1662 and 1674, is probably the most complete and useful of the earlier taxes. It required householders to pay a tax of two shillings on each hearth in the house. Not only do we have householders' names but we can also infer their status according to the number of hearths. The most complete set of records is for the tax collected on March 25, 1664. Many have been indexed and printed by local groups.

The Land Tax Redemption Office Quotas and Assessments for 1798-1799 are also valuable documents. All landowners in England and Wales are listed, town by town and village by village. Sadly it remains unindexed, making a location absolutely necessary beforehand.

d) Military records. The British Army has been a regularly organized body for several hundred years. Until the mid-nineteenth century, its organization was rather looser than we now associate with that institution, but it left a mass of records for the genealogist. The Army is divided into regiments, which were often associated with a county. There are four types of regiment:

    infantry   - foot soldiers
    cavalry   - horseback soldiers
    artillery - cannon-firers
    engineers - constructors of bridges, roads, etc.

Each regiment consists of commissioned officers, non-commissioned officers (who have risen from the ranks) and private soldiers. Commissions were bought and sold, a practice which effectively kept them within the domain of the upper classes.

The officer classes were, perhaps inevitably, better documented than the rank and file. Look first in the *Army Lists* published annually since 1754; a complete set is available at the Society of Genealogists. This will verify your ancestor's regiment(s) and career record. The P.R.O. has a regimental list of officers for the years 1702–1823 (WO 64). If there is any indication of involvement in campaigns, consult the Medal Rolls (WO 100) for details. Genealogical information can be gleaned from applications for commissions (WO 31) and widows' pensions (WO 42).

The career of the ordinary soldier is, alas, more difficult to reconstruct, and genealogical data is very limited. After 1883 discharge papers are arranged alphabetically regardless of regiment, thus easy to locate. Before that date, however, it is totally essential to know the man's regiment before consulting the War Office records, which run into the hundreds of thousands. If you think your ancestor served in a particular campaign, consult a military history to ascertain the regiments involved. One of my Irish ancestors supposedly served in the Crimea with great distinction, but so far I have been unable to locate any reference to him. It is my only clue, though, and I continue to be guided by it. Again, if medals were awarded to the ancestor, consult the Medal Rolls (WO 100). When you have found which regiment your ancestor belonged to, you can try searching the Regular Soldiers' Documents (WO 97) which detail soldiers' complete service record. The series runs from 1756 to 1913.

In the Naval records, officers are, again, much better documented than ratings are, and it is essential to know on which ship he served if he was in the Navy before 1853. Officer's careers have been published in the *Navy Lists* annually since 1814, and there are also many naval biographies such as *Commissioned Sea Officers of the Royal Navy, 1660-1815* (London, 1954). Primary sources such as the Captains Logs (ADM 51) may then be searched.

Unless his ship is known, a rating is very difficult to locate. Medal Rolls (ADM 171) can be of help. The Ship's Musters (ADM 36–39) give a great detail about the ratings' naval careers and even date and place of birth in some instances. These records survive from 1667 onwards. In the absence of a muster, Ship's Pay Books can confirm the man's presence aboard ship.

The Merchant seaman record holdings of the P.R.O. relate mainly to the years 1837-1857. They include Ship's Registers (1835-1857) and some muster rolls (1747-1834). Crew lists are accessible by reference to the Registers, but be warned that the system is complex after 1845 and you may want to leave this research to a professional.

The P.R.O. does not hold Royal Air Force records. Personnel records may be released to relatives only by applying to the R.A.F. Personnel Management Centre, Easter Ave., Barnwood, Gloucester GL4 7AN.

e) Records relating to British citizens abroad. Some registers of births, marriages, and deaths abroad were kept at various embassies and are now in the records of the Foreign Office at the P.R.O. Wills of Britons dying abroad were usually proven in the Prerogative Court of Canterbury and are therefore in the P.R.O. (See above.) These are records of many British nationals, not merely civil servants of Crown employees.

Births, marriages, and deaths at sea from 1854 to 1890 are among the records of the Board of Trade (BT 158). Deaths at sea of British nationals 1825-1880 are classified under BT 159, and births at sea 1875-1891 are in BT 160.

f) Emigrations records. Formal emigration lists have never been kept, but the following classes of documents might be useful to the American genealogist:

-BT 27 - Passenger Lists, 1890-1960; arranged by year and port of departure, they give the name, age, occupation and last address of the passenger.

-T 47/9-12 - Register of emigrants to America, 1773-1776, for which there is a card index. The index gives name, age, occupation, reason for leaving Britain, last address and destination.

-AO 12 - American Loyalists' Claims 1776-1831

-AO 13 - American Loyalists' Claims 1780-1835

g) Deeds. There are thousands of deeds in the Public Record Office but unfortunately there is no index to the majority of them. They are arranged in chronological order by the date of filing and there is a notation of the county in the margin. You may wish to hire a professional researcher if you are fairly confident that a deed exists and do not have the time to search on your own.

Two considerations need to be kept in mind. Firstly, that land and property ownership has until this century been the exclusive preserve of a very small class of English society. The chances that your ancestor held property are quite limited. Secondly, until the nineteenth century, there was no legal requirement to keep deeds or to record transfer of ownership. Most people held land by copyhold, a form of tenure now abolished, and transfers were recorded on the court roll of the manor. Most court rolls are held by the county record offices and many have been printed by archaeological societies.

h) Census returns. See Chapter 5.

i) Apprenticeship records. See Chapter 6.

What Not To Expect At The P.R.O. (Kew)

Formal genealogies
Anglican parish registers
Birth, marriage or death records
Wills after 1858
Records of soldiers serving in the Boer War, World Wars I or
    II.

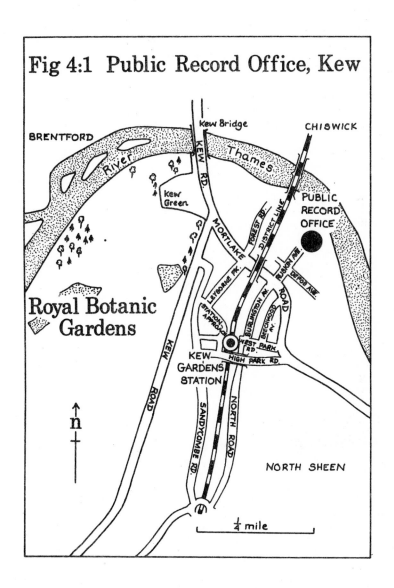

Fig 4:1 Public Record Office, Kew

CHAPTER 5

OTHER LONDON RECORD REPOSITORIES

<u>Land</u> <u>Registry</u> <u>Office</u> (Census branch of the Public Record Office)

Portugal Street
London WC2A 1LR
Telephone: 01-405-3488
Hours: 9:30 a.m. to 5:30 p.m. weekdays

The original copies of census records, taken every ten years from 1841 to 1881, are housed with the Domesday Book and other fragile materials at the P.R.O. in Chancery Lane. They are not available for use. Microfilm copies may be consulted, free of charge, at the Land Registry Office. If you do not have a P.R.O. reader's ticket, a day-pass can be obtained without a fuss at the entrance.

Be warned: this is a busy place! If you cannot arrive at the opening time, try the lunch hour. You may feel intimidated by the hoards of people who really look as if they know what they are doing, but you will soon feel like an old hand. Come prepared with as much information as possible about the families for whom you are searching. If they lived in a large town, have a street address. (Was the ancestor or a sibling born in a census year? Obtain the birth certificate for their residence.)

The Office has its own system for obtaining the microfilm needed and large posters hung on the walls explain what you need to do: a slip must be filled in with the correct reference numbers for the enumeration district, street, etc., which are to be found in indexes. Despite lack of time, try not to rush. Write legibly: preprinted forms prove very useful and time saving.

Censuses are probably the single most vital public record to genealogists. They should be used with care and intelligence. When searching an area for a surname, particularly a rare one, note all the individuals with that name. They may tie in later. Often it is important to have all the siblings' names in a family, in order to identify it definitely. Perhaps you see what you believe to be an enumerator's error; do not be tempted to correct it automatically. Later you may not remember whose error it was, or even that it was an error.

Some notes on British censuses:

Dates Taken:

7 June 1841
30 March 1851
8 April 1861
3 April 1871
4 April 1881

The 1841 census was the first, not destroyed, to record names. Ages in it are rounded to the nearest five years. Some abbreviations used:

/	end of one family
//	end of house
Y/N	Yes or No
N.K.	Not Known
Ind.	Independent means
J.	Journeyman
F.W.K.	Framework knitter
F.S./M.S.	Female or male servant
Agr. or Ag. Lab.	Agricultural Labourer

The 1851 & later censuses give:
    actual age
    place of birth
    relationship to head of household
    marital status

St. Catherine's House (birth & marriage certificates)

10 Kingsway
London WC2B 6JP
Telephone: 01-242-0262
Hours: 8:30 a.m. to 4:30 p.m. weekdays

The General Registry Office houses all the birth, marriage

48

and death records since they were legislated by Parliament – July 1st, 1837. Only the indexes are available directly to the public for consultation, and these occupy many hundreds of volumes in the Office's reading rooms. Actual certificates must be purchased when the appropriate entry has been located in the index.

The indexes are located on the ground floor of the building, which in American terms is the first floor. A new reading room has been built at the rear of the building and the marriage indexes are now housed there. These obviously take up much more space than the births and deaths, because for each marriage, two names are indexed. The indexes for the first quarter century or so after 1837 are handwritten and all the volumes are very large and heavy. Bring your own muscles. There is no place to sit but slanted reading tables at waist level run between the stacks.

Indexes for births, marriages and deaths are all arranged in basically the same format. Each calendar year is divided into four quarters, and each quarter may occupy several volumes. Within the quarter, names of all persons mentioned are in alphabetical order by surname and then by Christian name. The actual dates of the events are not given, only the registration district, volume and page number of the entry in the actual register. Remember that parents had 42 days to report a birth, so if it occurred near the end of a quarter, it might not appear until the next quarter.

DETAILS YOU CAN EXPECT TO FIND ON CERTIFICATES

Birth (Full Certificate)

Child's full name
Name of mother
Name of father
Occupation of father <u>or</u> status
Address
Date and time of birth

Birth (Short Certificate)

Child's full name
Date of birth

Marriage

Names of bride and groom

Their marital statuses
Their addresses at time of marriage
Names of the witnesses to the marriage (usually two)
Occupation or status of the couple
Place and date of ceremony
Whether marriage was after banns or with license

Death

Name and address of deceased
Place and time of death
Cause of death
Age of deceased
Name of attending doctor

The fee for a certificate is £4.60 and they take about 48 hours to prepare, so you can either return to St. Catherine's House and pick them up yourself or have them posted to your hotel.

Other indexes:

Births and deaths at sea: 1 July, 1837 to 31 December, 1874
British births abroad since 1 July, 1849
Army returns of births, marriages and deaths from 1761
Royal Air Force returns of births, marriages and deaths since 1920

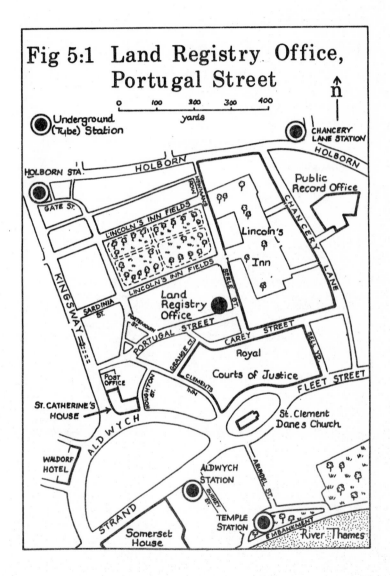

Fig 5:1 Land Registry Office, Portugal Street

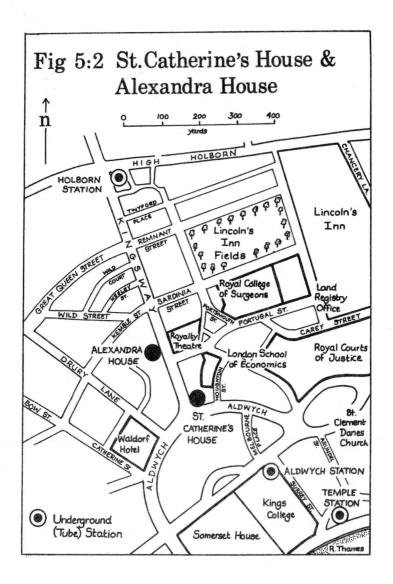

Fig 5:2 St. Catherine's House & Alexandra House

n

0   100   200   300   400
yards

HIGH   HOLBORN

HOLBORN
STATION

CHANCERY LA.

TWYFORD
PLACE

REMNANT
STREET

Lincoln's
Inn
Fields

Lincoln's
Inn

GREAT QUEEN STREET

WILD
COURT

KEELEY
ST.

KEMBLE ST.

SARDINIA
STREET

Royal College
of Surgeons

Land
Registry
Office

WILD STREET

KINGSWAY

PORTSMOUTH ST.

PORTUGAL ST.

CAREY   STREET

Royalty
Theatre

ALEXANDRA
HOUSE

DRURY LANE

London School
of Economics

HOUGHTON ST.

Royal Courts
of Justice

BOW ST.

ALDWYCH

ST.
CATHERINE'S
HOUSE

MELBOURNE PLACE

St.
Clement
Danes
Church

Waldorf
Hotel

CATHERINE S.

ALDWYCH

Underground
(Tube) Station

Kings
College

Somerset House

SURREY ST.

ARUNDEL

ALDWYCH STATION

TEMPLE
STATION

R. Thames

The Society of Genealogists

14, Charterhouse Buildings,
Goswell Road,
London EC1M 7BA
Tel: 01-251-8799
Hours: Closed Mondays. Open Tuesday, Friday, and Saturday
10 a.m. - 6 p.m. Wednesday and Thursday 10 a.m. - 8 p.m.

The Society of Genealogists has undoubtedly the most important collection of genealogical materials in the British Isles. It was founded in 1911 "to promote and encourage the study of genealogy" and although it once had the exclusive atmosphere of a London gentleman's club, it has now shaken off that image and has become a modern organization, ready and willing to help all family historians. The Society boasts the distinguished patronage of H.R.H. Prince Michael of Kent as its president, with the eminent genealogist A.J. Camp serving as director. In July 1984, the Society moved from the extremely cramped house it had always occupied in South Kensington to a new and modern facility in the East End. One does not have to be a member of the Society to use its extensive library. Fees are, however, charged to non-members on the following basis:

Ł2 for an hour
Ł5 for half a day
Ł7.50 for a day or a day and an evening.

These charges are very reasonable, especially when compared with the rates charged by professional genealogical researchers. The Society will also undertake research for non-members at a cost of $13.50 for an hour or $72 per day. A minimum of one or two days' work in advance is required, and you must be very specific about dates, names and places when setting research goals. The obvious advantage to this method is that the members who will do the research for you know the collection very well, to a degree that you, the outsider, cannot hope to match.

You may wish to consider membership in the Society, which costs $43 for the first year and $28 annually thereafter. Prospective members must find a proposer and seconder, preferably people who are already members, and each person's application is scrutinized before acceptance. In other words, membership is not automatic on paying of dues. You will receive the Society's quarterly, *Genealogist's Magazine*, obtain Society publications at a discount, and also be entitled to a lower research fee. You may also wish to subscribe to a quarterly newsletter, *Computers in Genealogy*, for Ł5 a year. Meetings are held regularly.

1) Parish register transcripts. This category covers baptismal, marriage and burial records of the Church of England. The Society has <u>no</u> original registers, but it does house about 8,000 transcripts. Some are complete copies, others are only extracts. They usually cover the period 1538 to 1812 or 1837, but some cover the later nineteenth century. A complete listing of the parishes for which copies are held is found in *Parish Register Copies: Society of Genealogists Collection*, obtainable from the Society for Ł2.80. Occasionally you will find a Bishop's Transcript, or BT, instead of the original register. These were exact copies of registers which the local priest was supposed to send to his bishop periodically, and often they have served to cover gaps in the originals. But remember, a BT transcript is a copy of a copy, and there has been more room for error to creep in. Invaluable as register transcripts are, they should be used with great care, and the original register should always be consulted as confirmation of your findings, even if only by mail. The transcripts at the Society are arranged by county, and interspersed with them are local histories, publications of local record and archaeological societies of the county.

There are also about 600 nonconformist register transcripts in the collection.

2) Directories and poll books. City and county directories have been published in Britain for several centuries and the Society has a large collection. Most directories will list only people of some substance - tradesmen, landowners, factory owners, clergy and professional men. Well-to-do widows are also listed in general. Occupation and street address are usually given. The Society also has clergy and medical directories. Poll books were lists of people eligible to vote and can be helpful, but bear in mind that prior to the Reform Acts of 1832 and 1864, the franchise was given to relatively few property-owners.

3) Army and Navy lists. The Army Lists are a type of military directory, published annually since 1754. Each edition lists all the officers currently serving in the armed forces and gives an account of his career to date, including regiment,

ranks held, battles and any medals awarded. The Society possesses a complete run of these and the Navy Lists, which is the seafaring equivalent. There is also an annual R.A.F. List but as it is of post-World War 1 origin, it may not be of much interest to the genealogist.

4) Calendars of wills before 1858. Calendars are lists or indexes of documents – in this case, wills. Prior to 1858, probate was an ecclesiastical matter and wills were proved in either the Prerogative Court of Canterbury (Southern counties) – abbreviated to P.C.C.; or the Prerogative Court of York (Northern counties) – abbreviated to P.C.Y. All the original P.C.C. wills are in the Public Record Office at Kew; the P.C.Y. will are in the Borthwick Institute in York. In a minority of cases, when the deceased lived in a special type of parish called a peculiar, the will was proved in the archdeacon's court and will be found in the County Record Office.

The P.C.C. wills are kept in large bound volumes and until 1841 the volumes were marked not by their year but by the first name in it. The individual will was then identified by a number, which is the folio number. A folio is a group of pages, possibly up to sixteen, so it is necessary to search all the pages in the folio until the correct will is located.
Example: Trenley, 178 indicates the register for 1742, folio 178.

Names of the P.C.C. registers of wills:

Abbott, 1729	Aylett, 1655
Abercrombie, 1801	Ayloffe, 1517
Adderley,	Babington, 1568
Adeane, 1506	Bakon, 1579
Alchin, 1654	Bargrave, 1774
Alen, 1546	Barnes, 1712
Alenger, 1540	Barrett, 1708
Alexander, 1775	Barrington, 1628
Anstis, 1744	Bath, 1680
Arden, 1840	Beard, 1830
Arran, 1759	Bedford, 1732
Arundell, 1580	Bellas, 1776
Ash, 1704	Bence, 1676
Aston, 1714	Bennett, 1508
Auber, 1730	Berkley, 1656
Audley, 1632	Bettesworth, 1752

Bevor, 1791
Bishop, 1790
Blamyr, 1501
Bodfelde, 1523
Bogg, 1769
Bolein, 1603
Bolton, 1724
Bond, 1696
Bowyer, 1652
Box, 1694
Boycott, 1743
Brent, 1653
Bridport, 1814
Brodrepp, 1738
Brook, 1728
Browne, 1740
Browning, 1719
Bruce, 1664
Brudenell, 1585
Bucke, 1551
Buckingham, 1721
Bunce, 1674
Busby, 1751
Butts, 1583
Byrde, 1624
Caesar, 1763
Calvert, 1788
Cambell, 1642
Cann 1685
Capell, 1613
Carew, 1576
Carr 1667
Chaynay, 1559
Chayre, 1563
Cheslyn, 1761
Clarke, 1625
Cobham, 1597
Coke, 1669
Coker, 1693
Collier, 1777
Collingwood, 1810
Collins, 1780
Coode, 1550
Cope, 1616
Cornwallis, 1783
Cottle, 1682

Coventry, 1640
Crane, 1643
Cresswell, 1818
Crickitt, 1811
Crumwell, 1536
Crymes, 1565
Dale, 1621
Daper, 1572
Darcy, 1581
Daughtry, 1577
Degg, 1703
Derby, 1736
Dixy, 1594
Dodwell, 1793
Dogett, 1491
Dorset, 1609
Drake, 1596
Drax, 1683
Drury, 1590
Ducarel, 1785
Ducie, 1735
Duke, 1671
Dycer, 1675
Dyer, 1701
Dyke, 1690
Dyngeley, 1537
Edmunds, 1746
Eedes, 1706
Effingham, 1817
Ellenboro', 1819
Ely, 1808
Ent, 1689
Erskine, 1824
Essex, 1648
Eure, 1672
Evelyn, 1641
Exeter, 1797
Exton, 1688
Fagg, 1715
Fairfax, 1649
Fane, 1692
Farquhar, 1833
Farrant, 1727
Fenner, 1612
Fetiplace, 1511
Fines, 1647

Foot, 1687
Fountain, 1792
Fox, 1716
Gee, 1705
Glazier, 1756
Gloucester, 1835
Goare, 1637
Godyn, 1463
Gostling, 1782
Greenly, 1750
Grey, 1651
Hale, 1677
Hare, 1684
Harrington, 1592
Harris, 1796
Harte, 1604
Harvey, 1639
Hay, 1778
Hayes, 1605
Heathfield, 1813
Heber, 1827
Hele, 1626
Henchman, 1739
Hene, 1668
Herne, 1702
Herring, 1757
Herschell, 1822
Heseltine, 1804
Hogen, 1533
Holder, 1514
Holgrave, 1504
Holman, 1794
Holney, 1571
Horne, 1496
Howe, 1799
Hudleston, 1607
Hutton, 1758
Hyde, 1665
Irby, 1695
Isham, 1731
Jankyn, 1529
Jenner, 1770
Juxon, 1663
Kent, 1820
Kenyon, 1802
Ketchyn, 1556

Kidd, 1599
King, 1679
Lane, 1709
Langley, 1578
Laud, 1662
Lawe, 1614
Lee, 1638
Leeds, 1713
Legard, 1767
Leicester, 1588
Lewyn, 1597
Lisle, 1749
Liverpool, 1829
Lloyd, 1686
Loftes, 1561
Logge, 1479
Lort, 1698
Loveday, 1809
Luffenam, 1423
Lushington, 1807
Lynch, 1760
Lyon, 1570
Macham, 1789
Major, 1787
Mansfield, 1821
Marche, 1401
Marlbro, 1722
Marriott, 1803
Martyn, 1574
May, 1661
Maynwaryng, 1520
Meade, 1618
Mellershe, 1559
Mico, 1666
Milles, 1487
Montague, 1602
Moone, 1500
More, 1554
Morrison & Crynies, 1565
Nabbs, 1660
Nelson, 1805
Nevell, 1593
Newcastle, 1795
Nicholl, 1838
Noel, 1700
Noodes, 1558

Norfolk, 1786
North, 1681
Norwich, 1837
Ockham, 1734
Oxford, 1812
Pakenham, 1815
Parker, 1619
Paul, 1755
Pell, 1659
Pembroke, 1650
Penn, 1670
Peter, 1573
Pett, 1699
Pile, 1636
Pinfold, 1754
Pitt, 1806
Plymouth, 1726
Poley, 1707
Populwell, 1548
Porch, 1525
Potter, 1747
Powell, 1552
Price, 1733
Pye, 1673
Pykering, 1575
Pyne, 1697
Pynning, 1544
Reeve, 1678
Richards, 1823
Richmond, 1723
Ridley, 1629
Rivers, 1644
Rockingham, 1784
Romney, 1725
Rous, 1384
Rowe, 1583
Rudd, 1615
Rushworth, 1765
Russell, 1633
Ruthen, 1657
Rutland, 1588
Sadler, 1635
Sainberbe, 1591
St. Albans, 1825
St. Eloy, 1762
St. John, 1631

Savile, 1622
Scott, 1595
Scroope, 1630
Seager, 1634
Searle, 1753
Secker, 1768
Seymer, 1745
Shaller, 1720
Sheffelde, 1569
Simpson, 1764
Skinner, 1627
Smith, 1710
Soame, 1620
Spencer, 1587
Spert, 1541
Spurway, 1741
Stafford, 1606
Stevens, 1773
Stevenson, 1564
Stokton, 1454
Stonard, 1567
Stowell, 1836
Strahan, 1748
Streat, 1562
Sutton, 1828
Swabey, 1826
Swann, 1623
Tashe, 1553
Taverner, 1772
Tebbs, 1831
Teignmouth, 1834
Tenison, 1718
Tenterden, 1832
Thower, 1531
Tirwhite, 1582
Trenley, 1742
Trevor, 1771
Twisse, 1646
Tyndall, 1766
Vaughan, 1839
Vere, 1691
Vox, 1493
Wake, 1737
Wallop, 1600
Walpole, 1798
Warburton, 1779

Watson, 1584
Wattys, 1471
Webster, 1781
Weldon, 1617
Welles, 1558
Whitfield, 1717
Windebanck, 1608
Windsor, 1586

Wingfield, 1610
Wood, 1611
Woodhall, 1601
Wootton, 1658
Wrastley, 1557
Wynne, 1816
Young, 1711

The Society of Genealogists holds the three indexes to P.C.C. wills.

5) Boyd's Marriage Index. Percival Boyd was an eminent member of the Society of Genealogists who, before the age of the micro-chip and word processor, decided to compile an index of all the marriages in England from 1538 to which he could have access. This was, indeed, a lifetime's work and was still nowhere near completion when Mr. Boyd died in 1955. He had read through all the printed parish registers and transcripts at the society and for each made an index slip. At certain stages, he compiled his findings into typed volumes. There are three series of volumes to the Boyd's Marriage Index:

First Series. This was compiled on a county basis. Since Boyd had access only to printed registers, many parishes were not included, or only portions of a register, if it was abstracted. If there is an M̲ on the spine, men's names only are indexed in the volume; W̲ means women's names indexed; – indicates a mixed index; M̲W̲ means both men's and women's names are indexed, but separately. Within each volume, the time span is divided into ten periods. Counties covered in the first series are:

Cambridgeshire
Cornwall
Cumberland
Derbyshire
Devon
Durham
Essex
Gloucestershire

Lancashire
London and Middlesex
Norfolk
Northumberland
Somerset
Staffordshire
Suffolk
Yorkshire

Second series. This is known as the Miscellaneous Marriage Index and covers 1538–1837 only. It indexes printed calendars of marriage licenses, marriages mentioned in *Gentleman's Magazine* (a 'society' periodical), and counties not in the first series. However, the series is not arranged by county.

Third series. An alphabetical index of over one million names left over after Mr. Boyd's death and not included by him in the first two series. They were arranged by the Genealogical Society of Salt Lake City into alphabetical order.

Each reference to a marriage in the three series consists of only one line. For example, if you consulted the Norfolk Marriage Index Brides section for the late 18th century, letter G, you would find:

Year Female Male Where

1794 GUYTON, Easter (married to) Dunthorn, George Thursford.

For a fuller account of the ceremony, it would be necessary to consult the printed parish register at the Society of Genealogists or, preferably, the original, which in this case is held at the Norfolk County Record Office. This would give details of age, residence and marital status. Boyd's is an invaluable research tool but no substitute for the actual documentary source.

6) Printed and typescript family histories and genealogies. The Society has a large collection, comprising volumes presented by members and those acquired by purchase.

7) London 'Society' periodicals and newspapers. In this category are included publications such as *Gentleman's Magazine*, which began in 1731 as a chronicle of the main social events in the lives of the upper classes - betrothals, "coming out" into society, weddings, bereavements, and so forth. Each annual volume is indexed, by surname only, though there are cumulative indexes for 1731-1786 and 1786-1810. Marriages are indexed to 1768 and biographical notices and obituaries are indexed to 1780. Obituaries from *The Times* are also kept.

8) Pedigrees submitted to the Society.

9) Records of the East India Company. The East India Company was begun in 1601 strictly as a trading company, but in the 18th century began to expand it powers in India in such a way that by the India Act of 1784 it actually became the

government of India. It had two classes of employees, both British emigrès: merchants, who were recompensed with their profits; and civil servants, who worked for a salary. The Company's position declined after the Indian Mutiny of 1857, which caused India to come directly under the rule of the Crown, but for almost two centuries it kept records of the British men and their families who served it. Further information can be found in G. Hamilton-Edward's *In Search of Ancestry*, London, Phillimore, 1974 (new edition).

10) The Great Slip Index: 800 boxes of indexed biographical material collected by the Society, containing about three million references.

11) The International Genealogical Index (I.G.I.) contains references to millions of baptisms and other events throughout the world, but mainly in England and Wales. The Index is on microfiche and is continually being updated.

Principle Probate Registry

Somerset House,
Strand, London WC2R 1LP
Tel: 01-405-7641
Hours: 10 a.m.- 4:30 p.m., Monday-Friday

Somerset House, as it is generally known, houses all wills from January 11, 1858. The wills are all indexed, as are letters of administration, which give details of how the estates of those who died intestate were disposed of. From 1858 to 1870, wills and administrations were indexed in separate volumes, but as the labeling on the spines is not very distinct, be sure you have checked the correct volume. Copies of wills can be obtained for 25p (about 40) each. Originals of wills can be consulted without charge, but you may not copy out the contents word for word!

The Principal Probate Registry also accepts postal applications for searches. Write and ask for form PR100. You will need to know the deceased person's surname, forenames, date of death and address at time of death. The total cost is Ł2 (about $3), which is non-refundable even if no will is found. Payment should be made by international money order, available from banks, and in pounds sterling.

Post-1858 wills can be most useful, not only in clarifying the various relationships within a family, but also because specific addresses are given which can lead to results when searching the censuses.

The British Library

a) Reading Room at the British Museum, Great Russell St.
   Telephone: 01-363-1544
   Hours: Monday through Saturday 9:00 a.m. to 5:00 p.m.

The Reading Room of the British Museum is the equivalent of the U.S. Library of Congress. It houses virtually every book ever published in Britain, including local histories and biographies, perhaps even books written by your ancestor. Many, of course, are rare and you may find a long sought-after genealogy or city directory. Make out a list beforehand of what you hope to locate.

It is necessary to apply for a reader's ticket well in advance. If you are not absolutely sure you will be visiting the Reading Room, do not hesitate to apply for a card anyway - better to be safe than sorry.

b) Newspaper Library
   Colindale Ave., London NW9
   Telephone: 01-205-6039 or -4788

All nineteenth and twentieth century newspapers, provincial and foreign before 1800 are housed at the Newspaper Library. As you can imagine, the volume of material is staggering, so it is essential to have a specific date and location for your search. You will fill in a request slip and a page will bring you the papers from the stacks.

Newspapers are a very useful tool for the genealogist, capable of providing information which might otherwise have gone unrecorded. This is particularly true of obituaries. My grandmother's revealed that my grandfather had been a city councillor and she had therefore been given a civic funeral.

LDS Branch Library

64-68 Exhibition Road
London SW 2
Telephone: 01-589-8561

Located conveniently near the South Kensington underground station, the LDS Library has the microfiche I.G.I., standard English genealogical reference books, and microfilm of many parish registers.

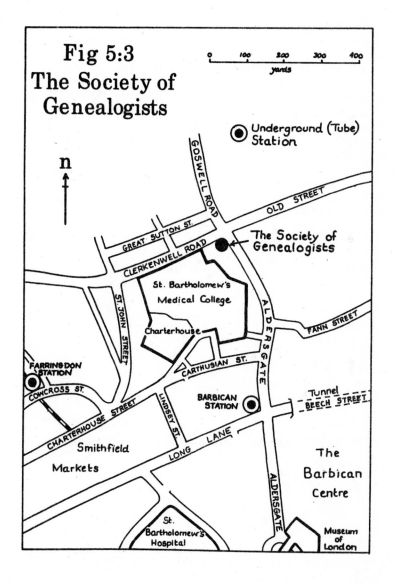

Fig 5:3
The Society of
Genealogists

0   100   200   300   400
yards

⊙ Underground (Tube) Station

n

GOSWELL ROAD

OLD STREET

GREAT SUTTON ST.

CLERKENWELL ROAD

The Society of Genealogists

St. Bartholomew's Medical College

Charterhouse

ST. JOHN STREET

ALDERSGATE

FANN STREET

CARTHUSIAN ST.

FARRINGDON STATION

COWCROSS ST.

CHARTERHOUSE STREET

LINDSEY ST.

BARBICAN STATION ⊙

Tunnel
BEECH STREET

Smithfield Markets

LONG LANE

The Barbican Centre

ALDERSGATE

St. Bartholomew's Hospital

Museum of London

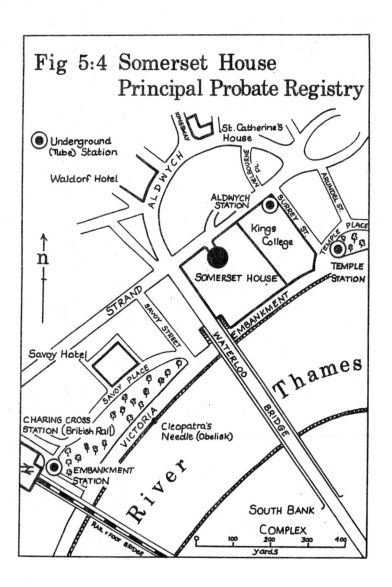

Fig 5:4 Somerset House Principal Probate Registry

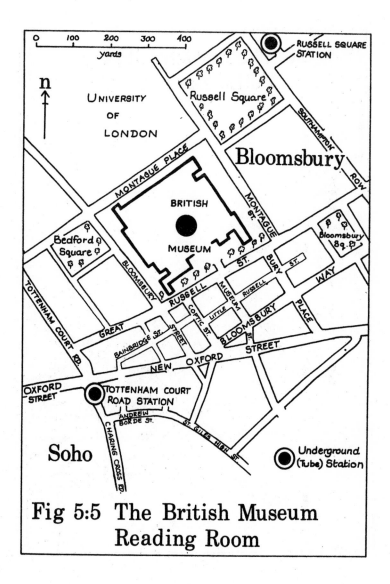

Fig 5:5 The British Museum
Reading Room

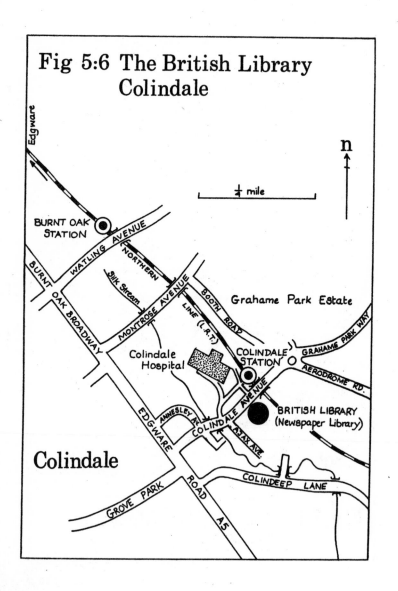

Fig 5:6 The British Library
Colindale

CHAPTER 6

RESEARCH IN AND AROUND THE PARISH CHURCH

The parish is probably the most ancient unit of ecclesiastical and civil administration in England. Parishes had almost certainly evolved by 1066 and many stand today in the boundaries they occupied in 1291. Thomas Cromwell, Henry VIII's Vicar-General, was the first to hint at a civil or administrative use of the parish when he instituted the registering of baptisms, marriages, and burials.

The Poor Law Act of 1601 created the 'civil' parish, which usually corresponded to the ecclesiastical one, and gave the parish council or 'vestry' new powers and obligations, which mainly concerned the care of the poor and indigent, thus creating a series of records about a class of society which would otherwise be undocumented.

Many of the parishes have deposited all their records at their county or diocesan record office, especially since the General Synod of the Church of England passed its 1978 measure requiring archival-quality depositories for such documents, but many still remain in the parishes. Fees or a donation are asked for searches.

Main Types of Parish Record of Use to Genealogists

a) Baptism, marriage and burial registers. Until the 19th century, baptisms, burials, and marriages were generally entered in one book, rather mixed and not easily searched. Very early registers may be in Latin. To determine the earliest date for which registers survive in your parish, consult A. M. Burke's, *Key to the Ancient Parish Registers of England and Wales.* Note that all marriages had to be performed in the Church of England, except Jews and Quakers, hence many Catholics and Non-conformists held two ceremonies.

b) Banns books: after 1753. "Banns" refers to the notice of marriage called out in the parishes of the couple for three consecutive weeks before the wedding. These may give more information than the marriage register, but remember that the marriage may not necessarily have taken place! (Before 1753, banns were usually recorded in the register.)

c) Ratepayers' lists: "Rates" are the English equivalent of property taxes and so ratepayers' lists will show the names of those who owned property within the parish.

d) Vestry minutes. The vestry was the ruling body of the parish, a group of men elected or appointed to run the affairs of the parish. After the passing of the Elizabethan Poor Law, their duties became much more civic and less ecclesiastical, having to deal with the poor parishioners, vagrants, apprenticeships and much more. In many cases, the vestry had a very hard-headed attitude, almost un-Christian, refusing shelter and care to those for whom it did not have a legal responsibility. The vestry appointed church wardens, parish constables (fore-runners of the police), and overseers of the poor. All these officials reported regularly to the vestry. W.E.Tate, author of *The Parish Chest*, states that "vestry minutes are among the most interesting of parish records." Particularly if your ancestor was from the working, agricultural or servant classes of society, you may be lucky enough to find many references to their upkeep.

e) Records of the Overseers of the Poor include:

-settlement certificates, which were in effect passports for paupers. A pauper - that is, a person with no visible means of support such as a trade - had to have proof of his parish of origin, usually the parish where he was born or apprenticed, in order to be accepted in another parish. If he ever became reliant on the poor law provisions, he would be returned to his settlement parish. On arrival at the new parish, the pauper handed his settlement certificate to the vestry. Settlement certificates may show if any other family members accompanied the pauper and what age they were.

-account books. Up to 1834 (when the new Poor Law Act was passed) the account books are extremely detailed. All moneys disbursed were accounted for in detail, and such items as fathers of bastards, apprenticeship arrangements for pauper children, and vagrant passes are often mentioned.

f) Apprenticeship records, mainly after 1757. Pauper children were apprenticed at cost to the parish and apprenticeship constituted legal 'settlement' in the parish. Apprenticeship indentures give name of child and age, and domicile, name, parish, and trade of master, and years of indenture.

When a parish issued a certificate of settlement, it acknowledged its obligation to give relief to the recipient if they became a pauper. The settlement parish might not be the recipient's present address, but where he or she would be sent if impoverished.

g) Burial-in-woolen certificates (1666-1814). In 1666, Parliament enacted a law requiring burial in woolen and a certificate to show it, to promote Britain's flagging wool industry. Within eight days of burial, someone present at the funeral had to furnish the affidavit - stating that the corpse's shroud had been woolen. Enforcement of the law did lapse some time before its repeal in 1814.

h) Censuses. As noted in Chapter 4, the earlier national censuses (1801-1831) were taken by the parish constables and although they were supposed to have been destroyed after all the computations were made, many constables copied their own returns into the vestry minutes or registers. An inquiry on this matter is certainly worthwhile.

Other documents that list all male citizens are:

-the poll-tax lists. Poll ("head") taxes were levied on all men over sixteen in 1641, 1660, 1666 and 1677. In parishes where the lists survive, they can be very useful as they often describe the relationships between people on the list, presumably to distinguish them.

-the 1641 Protestation Returns. At the beginning of the English Civil War, Parliament was very nervous of pro-Royalist feelings in the country and so ordered every male of 18 years or older to take an oath "protesting" his loyalty to the Parliamentary cause and to sign his name (or make his mark) to that effect. Almost all did so, and lists were also made of those who refused. The original returns are in the Record Office of the House of Lords but parishes sometimes kept their own copy. The lists are not easy to read, but by no means impossible with some study.

i) Tithe award maps. The custom of "tithing", giving one-tenth of one's income to the local priest, had begun in England as far back as the eighth century, but after the Reformation in the sixteenth century money payments were usually substituted for payments in kind. The effect of land enclosure and the Agrarian Revolution in the eighteenth century was the need to formalize the tithing system into a type of property tax. Therefore, the early nineteenth century saw many parishes being surveyed by Tithe Commissioners, who produced highly detailed Tithe Award maps, showing exactly who owned what and how much they owed as tithe. The scale on the maps is often as large as 10 miles to 1 inch. Accompanying the maps was a description, giving the name of a field or building, its owner and its occupier (if different).

j) Touching for the King's Evil. In 1626 an Act required a patient wishing to be touched by the King to bring a certificate from his priest and churchwardens stating he had not been 'touched' before. These certificates named the patient, and his parents or spouse. The custom was discontinued by George I in 1714.

k) Sketch-maps of pew arrangements were often made to settle arguments between rival claimants. Nearness to the altar indicated high social standing; though not of strict genealogical importance, such knowledge is nevertheless an interesting dimension to the family history.

Outside The Church

Unlike churches in the U.S., English churches are usually surrounded by the graveyard, another valuable source of information. However, only a small percentage of Englishmen have had headstones erected, these being the wealthier elements of society, so do not expect 100% success in locating relevant tombstones. It is certainly worth a try, though. High boots or old shoes will be handy, for the ground may be muddy and nettles high.

To increase the legibility of a headstone, a safe and easy method is to take with you a container of shaving cream. Apply the cream liberally to the surface of the stone , then wipe across with a ruler or rag. You will find that the shaving-cream will have entered the crevices where the monument was inscribed, making the writing much more easily visible. The cream can then be completely wiped off, without any damage to the stone.

70

Transcribe the inscription <u>carefully</u> - guesses are worse than useless. Make some notes describing the exact location of the stone in relation to, say, the main entrance of the church or a lych-gate or tree. If time permits, make a sketch-map of the location of each stone recorded.

You may wish to photograph the stone as a permanent record. A 35mm camera with adjustable focus and variable shutter speeds is best, using a slow black and white film. Color film has an estimated life of only 50 years and should not be used if you want your negatives to last. Use a flash if the light is poor.

Have the camera parallel to the stone; do not shoot from a standing position. Most importantly, practice before your trip (in varying lighting conditions), in your local cemetery. Eliminate the chance of error on "the big day" when you find the headstone of your umpteenth great-grandfather!

Inside The Church

Take some time to explore the interior of the church. In particular, look for the following:

-monumental brasses. About 3,000 churches in England have at least one brass, which range in date from the 13th to the 18th centuries. Before the advent of the parish register, brasses recorded pictorially and with inscriptions the lives of the more prosperous members of the community - merchants, aldermen, knights, and gentry. You will find interesting depictions of contemporary costume, and the number of wives and children of the deceased may be shown in picture form. Brasses can often be rubbed, with the permission of the parish priest, but the proper cobbler's wax and paper must be used. It is increasingly the trend for churches to provide hobbyists with replicas of their brasses, to prevent further wear on the originals.

-tombstone effigies, possibly with heraldic devices to identify the deceased. Many are medieval, most are not later than the seventeenth century. Again, there will be little or nothing that may extend your lineage, but what could be more fascinating than gazing on the face of an ancestor dead for so many hundreds of years?

- memorial tablets, similar to tombstones but often with greater biographical detail, can be found decorating the walls.

71

-rolls of honour, usually commemorating soldiers from the Boer War (1899-1902#), World War I and World War II. These give the soldier's full name, rank and regiment, and sometimes the battle where the man met his death. This can certainly be a lead to documentary evidence at the P.R.O.

-parish or local history leaflets. It is impossible to trace your family history without some understanding of national and local events which shaped their lives, and a parish history can fill in many details for you. An excellent example of a longer work is the history of St. Godwald's Parish, Aston Fields, Worcestershire, by Janet Grierson and published by the parish. It shows how inextricably the life of the church was tied into that of the community and shows the evolution of the parish from a chapelry of Stoke Prior to an independent parish with the coming of the railway. Even briefer histories can be most illuminating.

DATES IMPORTANT IN DEVELOPMENT OF THE PARISH

1538 - Thomas Cromwell ordered that parish registers be kept on paper.

1558 - Accession of Elizabeth I. More registers survive from this date.

1559 - Act of Uniformity begins punishment of Roman Catholics and non-conformists.

1598 - Elizabeth I's church synod orders that registers be copied on vellum, from 1538, but many priests copy only from 1558.

1601 - Poor Law enacted - parishes become responsible for the maintenance of paupers.

1649 - 1660 - Interregnum under Cromwell. Most registers not kept.

1662 - Poor Law "Settlement" Act. Paupers must have settlement certificates if they wish to move.

1753 - Lord Hardwicke's Marriage Act: registers now kept in pre-printed books, with separate banns books.

1812 - Rose's Act: parish registers to be kept in three separate books.

1834 - New Poor Law ends the responsibility and power of the vestry.

1836 - Great Tithe Act leads to drawing up of Tithe Award maps.

1888 - Local Government Acts end the parish's civic responsibility totally.

CHAPTER 7

THE FAMILY HISTORY SOCIETY:
TO JOIN OR NOT TO JOIN?

England is very fortunate to be served by over sixty local family history and genealogical societies. Hardly any part of the country is without a group to which you can turn for help, and some more populous counties can boast several societies. The oldest, the Society of Genealogists, is based in London with worldwide membership and has a long and scholarly history. For many years the Society was run on the lines of a gentleman's club, but with the burgeoning interest in genealogy since the 1960's, it has dusted off its image, opened itself up and has even moved from its venerable but cramped quarters in Kensington to a more spacious and utilitarian building in the East End of London. Membership applications must be supported by two sponsors, preferably members themselves, or by professional persons of your acquaintance. The cost is $43 for the first year, $28 per annum thereafter. If you do not wish to join the Society but would like to subscribe to *The Genealogists' Magazine* (quarterly), you may do so at a cost of $20 per annum.

Locally-based societies are a great deal smaller than the Society of Genealogists; annual membership fees range from $10 to $15 for overseas members. The emphasis among these groups is family history, a broader-based subject than genealogy, but with genealogical research as its firm foundation.

What do you get for you money? Newsletters, interest and publication lists, and more.

All societies issue newsletters and journals, quarterly. The Norfolk and Norwich Genealogical Society's quarterly, *The Norfolk Ancestor* is a sixteen page journal, with a professional appearance. Members are also sent a hard-cover annual work, such as tax returns or parish records. The Birmingham and Midland Society for Genealogy and Heraldry publishes *The Midland Ancestor* quarterly, a forty page journal with regular columns such as "Bookworm" and "Census Strays", as well as articles from members. Most newsletters and journals carry a query column, in which members place ads (free or for a small fee) to help find missing ancestors.

Another useful tool published by many groups is a members' interest list. Members submit lists of surnames in which they are interested, and the reader can scan the list and write to members with whom he or she has a common interest. It would be very useful to establish communication with such people well before a planned visit to England, not only to enlist their aid but to establish a working relationship which could reach fruition during the visit.

According to the size of the society, it will have a smaller or larger publications list. These could include a local genealogical records guide, parish register transcripts, census indexes, monument inscriptions, maps, plus publications of national societies.

These publications are generally unavailable except through the society and as they are in relatively small editions, they become rare and worth their weight in gold.

For the person visiting England, there is access to genealogical society libraries. The size and quality of the collection will vary tremendously, depending on the society. One library I visited was in the chairman's cellar and had a very higgledy-piggledy aspect: there was a card catalogue, and even a section of the I.G.I., but the chairman was the only person able to locate material. Fortunately, he was obliging and helpful. Another society library I used was housed in the basement of an educational institution, was well organized, and had on duty a volunteer to help members find what they needed.

Some larger societies have established postal lending libraries. This can be expensive but may be worth inquiring about. Generally, the lending library catalog is much shorter than the regular library's catalog.

The Birmingham and Midland Society goes a step further in helping new members by assigning each a correspondence secretary, to whom the new member can write with any questions or problems. This is an innovation which should be applauded and imitated.

The overseas member can benefit enormously through entitlement to the Federation of Family History Societies Accommodation Register. Only F.H.S. Members may buy a copy, which lists other members in most counties willing to offer bed and breakfast. Not only do you "sleep cheap" (and probably in cozy comfort), but you also get to 'talk shop' and quite possibly benefit from your hosts' local knowledge. The advantages are obvious. Your copy may be obtained for $2.25 surface mail or $2.85 airmail from Mrs. C. Walcot, 1 Strode Manor Farm Cottages, Netherbury, Bridport, Dorset DTG 5NG. Quote your society and membership number.

Remember that English genealogical and family history societies were not established as pedigree societies, such as the Daughters of the American Revolution. They are manifestations of a keen interest in local history and a desire for self-knowledge.

NOTE: A complete list of Family History Societies with addresses is given in Appendix C.

CHAPTER 8

SOLVING SOME COMMON GENEALOGICAL PROBLEMS

This chapter will explore some of the more common and frustrating problems which you may encounter during your research trip. It will suggest some solutions and hope that these will lead you to create your own answers, or spot your mistakes.

Unable To Locate A Subject's Birth Certificate

-check that your source of information for place is correct. If in doubt, go to the census nearest to that date and check for a street address. Remember, too, that Registration Districts were changed in 1852.

-check diverse spellings of both Christian and surnames. Did the subject have two forenames originally? They may have been juxtaposed, so be careful.

-child may have been registered with a totally different Christian name. My great-grandmother was always known as Annie Elizabeth. I completely failed to locate her birth certificate, though I did find her baptismal record. Some time later a great-aunt told me she had been registered as Harriet for some unknown reason, and so had had great difficulty proving, for social security reasons, her age!

-child may have been register with a different surname:
    a) if illegitimate
    b) to hide illegitimacy
    c) if later adopted

Illegitimacy led to a great deal of lying to the authorities. The father of author Barbara Pym stated on his marriage certificate that he was the son of Thomas Pym, farmer, deceased.

He was actually Thomas' grandson: his birth certificate showed he was the son of Phoebe Pym, a servant. No father's name was given on the certificate.

-registration was not compulsory until 1875 and many births were simply never registered.

-human error - did you read the indexes correctly or did you tire and miss some entries?

-cross-check with the I.G.I. and parish records.

-if you still cannot locate the child's entry, settle for that of a brother or sister. The same basic information will be given.

Unable To Locate A Marriage Certificate

Marriage records can be difficult and tedious to locate at St. Catherine's House if you are searching a common name, or if your information is incomplete; e.g., missing the bride's first and maiden name. There are, however, other reasons for failure.

-are the names of the parties correct? Check various spellings and any aliases; e.g., name by a previous marriage, or adoption.

-could they have married elsewhere? Check adjacent parishes and nearby large cities. My grandmother married in a Birmingham church though she lived in the parish of Clent.

-check other years. People have often falsified statements orally and in family bibles to hide a 'shot-gun wedding'.

-are you sure a wedding ever took place? Even if its intent was recorded in banns books or a license issued, this does not mean for certain that it happened.

-human error - did you read carefully enough?

-human error - was the marriage wrongly indexed? Try to imagine the possibilities.

-censuses - check where the first child was born. This could provide a valuable clue to the place and time of the marriage.

Unable To Locate A Death Certificate

-start at the latest possible date. This can be established from the censuses, or at least ninety years after the birth date. Work backwards, always bearing in mind the person's age.

-if the subject was widowed, she may have remarried and died under a different name. Check the marriage indexes.

-did the person possibly die abroad or in military service? St. Catherine's has separate registers for deaths at sea and abroad. The War Office has a list of deaths during World War I, and earlier Armed Services records are in the Public Record Office.

-check at the Principal Probate Registry for a will. This would help pinpoint a date and place of death.

-human error - have you read the indexes carefully enough.

-human error - the information on death certificates can only be as good as the informant. This may not have been a close relative; errors in spellings and facts can ensue.

-alternative sources of information include burial registers, undertakers' records, obituaries and monumental inscriptions.

Mother's Maiden Name Not Known

Try to locate a marriage certificate or record:

a) check the I.G.I. in London; this is housed in Exhibition Road and the Society of Genealogists.

b)check the Pallot Index. This covers the years 1780-1837 and is especially strong for the London marriages (101 of 103 ancient parishes have been covered); forty English counties are also included. The Pallot Index is housed at the Institute of Genealogical and Heraldic Studies in Canterbury. (See Appendix D.) There is a fee for each search.

c) check Boyd's marriage index, either at the L.D.S. library or the Society of Genealogists.

-did the subject or her husband of siblings leave a will? Check at the Principal Probate Registry. A will can give clues to her family's name and location.

-did the subject's children have any unusual middle names?

-check for the existence of a passport and re-check any family papers for clues you may have missed.

Failure To Find An Individual In The Census

The source of your address information, a certificate, newspaper clipping, etc., will very likely be out of date by the next census. You can:

-search a city directory of a date near to the census date.

-search the electoral rolls.

-if a small town, search its census records and those of adjacent towns. Be diligent, it can be very time consuming.

-human errors - on your part or that of the census-enumerator?

-check I.G.I., Boyd's, or the Pallot Index.

-could the person have lived in another household; for example, as a servant or visitor?

-a good knowledge of local and socioeconomic history might give clues as to the direction of migration. Wars, for example, have often had a profound effect on migration patterns.

When you come across an apparently insurmountable problem, do not feel defeated. Spread the facts out, sort them, analyze, and make a plan to get around the problem. Your answer may be buried deep in an index or a roll of microfilm, but if you do not look, you will never find it.

You Wish To Search One Of The Censuses 1891-1901

It is possible to obtain details of specific individuals named on censuses not yet released for general use. You must write to the Registrar General at St. Catherine's House, Kingsway, London W.I., enclosing £15. You must state your purpose and that the subject is either dead or assents to the search, and you must supply the exact address of the subject. (This can be obtained from a registrar's certificate, burial or baptismal record, or electoral rolls at the C.R.O.)

CHAPTER 9

INTERPRETING THE PAST

Interpretation Of Ancient Documents

Major obstacles in the reading of pre-nineteenth century records certainly exists for the genealogist unless he or she happens to have studied Latin and paleography. It is essential to study and be prepared before visiting archives or record offices; archivists are not there to be your personal record interpreter, that is your Job! I shall try to make the task lighter by taking each obstacle, step-by-step, and give exercises to help with each. Go over the exercises conscientiously and repeat them at intervals.

Spelling

We tend to take uniformity in spelling for granted, so you may be surprised to find out it is actually a very recent innovation. Before the nineteenth century and the movement towards public education, literate people were few and far between, and they tended to make up their own spelling as they wrote. It is not uncommon to find the same word spelled differently within the same sentence!

From my personal experience, I feel the best approach here is to use you imagination together with contextual clues. Hear the word as it would have been spoken, rather than trying to use the phonics rules you were taught in school, and ignore odd capital letters. All answers are at the end of the chapter.

Exercise 1A

Write the following phrases in modern English.

a) Itm one lynnen cloth
b) Itm one diapur Napkyn

c) Itm one Bason
d) Itm one Servyse boke
e) Itm one Surples, for the Person

Exercise 1B

Write the following phrases in modern English.

a) Elizabeth Smyth wyff of Jno was burried the xijth of Marche.
b) Anne borne of a wayfaringe woman was xd the xxth of Marche.
c) Jan Wagit wyff of Tho: was buryed the xxvith daye of Novembre.
d) Wyllm Dunkhorne and Merry hunt war Maried the xxth of April.

Archaic Terms

Archaic words are words no longer in use. Generally, the meaning of such words can be conjectured from the context of the piece. For example: "leasowe" which I discovered in the inventory of a seventeenth-century ancestor, I inferred meant "meadow" as the rest of the section was concerned with agricultural assets. The Oxford English Dictionary later confirmed my conjecture.

Below is a list of some other common archaic words. For words not listed here, refer to the Oxford English Dictionary which should be available at your library.

ambery/aumbry - small cupboard
band - 'bond', agreement
bandcloth - linen collar
beares, beres - pillowcases
bease - cattle
bed hillings - bedclothers
ben - hardware
chaffingdish - cooking dish
cordwood - firewood
deyhouse - dairy
form - bench
fustian - type of cloth
gawne - gallon pail
hogshead - 54 gallons
hutch - small chest for clothes

84

keep – a safe
lather – ladder
leasowe – meadow
press – cupboard – wardrobe
pullen – poultry
quern – hand–mill
spence – larder
tramells – instrument for lowering & raising a kettle over a
    fire
trestells – a beam
trivett – a three legged cooking stand
trussing bed – trendle bed
twilleys – woolen material
virginals – small harpsichord
whitch – coffer

Abbreviations And Contractions

Because wills, registers, and legal documents were
couched in jargon, it became the common practice to use
abbreviations and contractions for syllables and whole words.
These can be divided into several types.

1) Letters omitted completely – this was indicated by a mark
above the word, an apostrophe, or mark below the word.
Examples:

$\overline{\text{com}}$on – common
D$\overline{\text{m}}$i – Domini
Will$\overline{\text{m}}$ – William
$\overline{\text{M}}$garet – Margaret
$\underline{\text{p}}$fect – perfect
$\underline{\text{p}}$rede – precede
$\underline{\text{p}}$pose – propose
p'jury – perjury

2) Superior letters – the word is shortened by ommision of a
vowel and placing some of letters above the line. Examples:

w_{ch}^{th} – with
w^{ch} – which
we^{r} – were
y_{e} – that
y^{e} – the

85

Note: 'y' in the last two examples is a remnant of the Anglo-Saxon letter for 'th'.

3) Final letters ommitted - this is usually represented by a period, semi-colon, or colon. Examples:

> fro: - from
> wid. - widow
> ite; - item

4) Abbreviated names. Christian names were frequently abbreviated to save time, generally according to the rules above. Examples:

> J^{no} - John
> Rich^{r}d - Richard
> Robt - Robert
> Tho: - Thomas
> W^m - William
> Thoms - Thomas
> x̄pofer - Christopher
> Saml - Samuel
> Edwd - Edward

Handwriting

Handwriting has changed almost beyond recognition since the Tudor Age and can be the genealogist's greatest challenge.

It is not, however, an unsuperable one. Many English-speaking children learn to read and write fluently in Russian, Hebrew, and Greek, none of which uses the Roman alphabet. In paleography, we are using the Roman alphabet - the letter formations are simply different or more diverse than we, in the age of print, are used to.

1) The Secretary Alphabet

In Fig. 9A are given various common forms of each letter. Use a narrow calligraphic nib to copy each letter at least fifty times. When you are sure you know the letter forms, try writing the alphabet without reference to the model. Go back to Exercise 1 and write them out using your new skills.

GENERAL ALPHABET

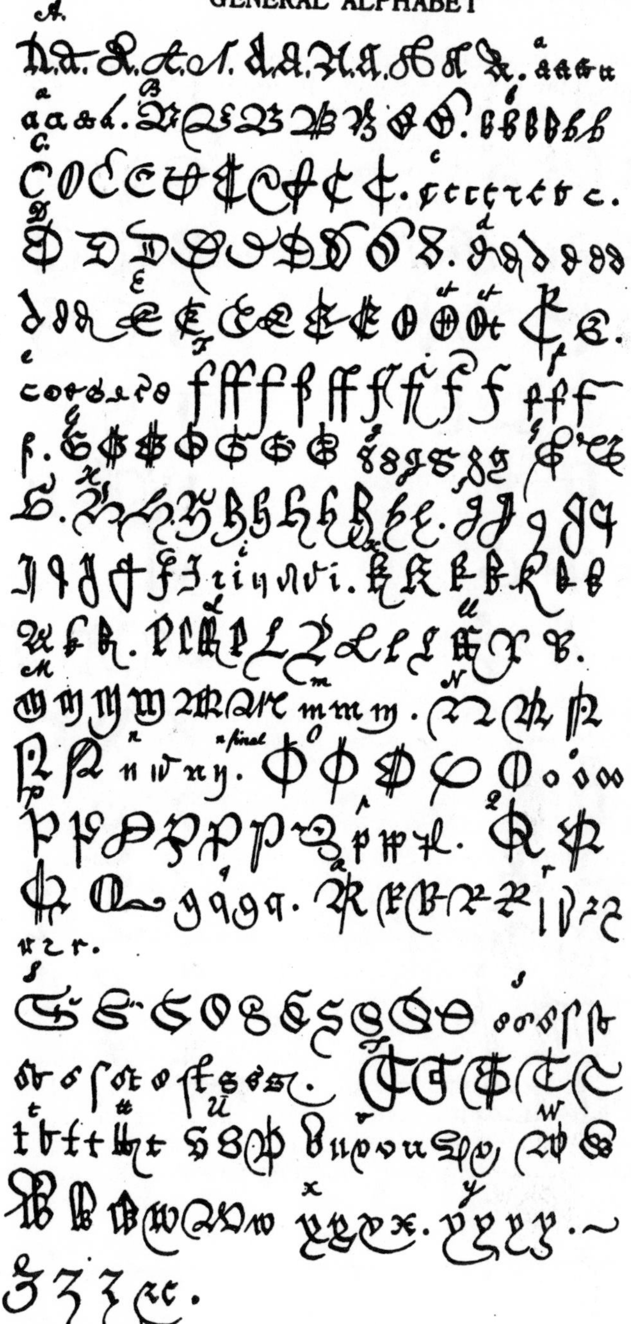

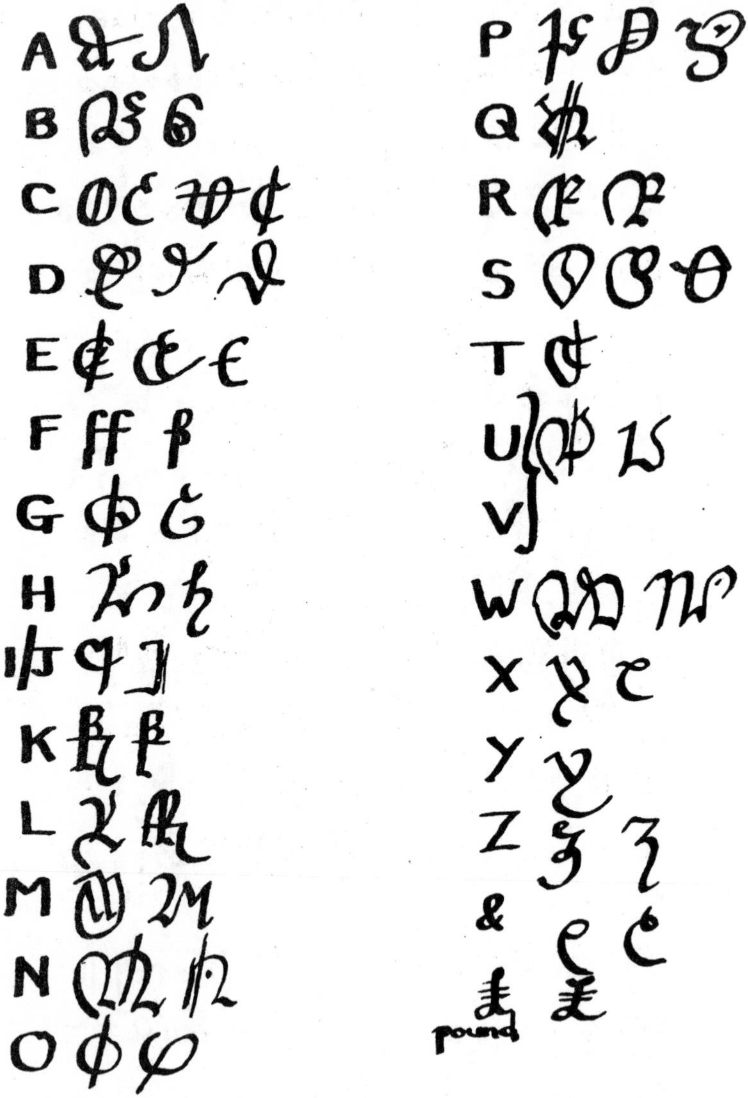

Fig. 9A

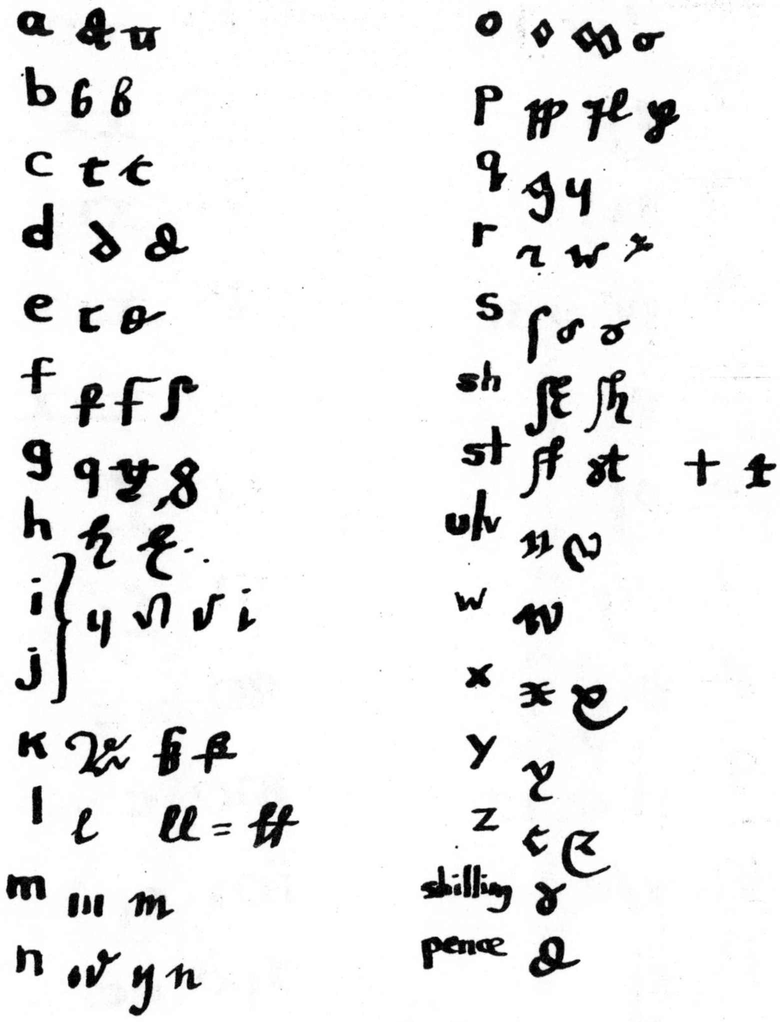

Fig. 9A

NUMERALS

1	i or j	15	xv
2	ij	20	xx
3	iij	21	xxj
4	jv or iv	25	xxv
5	v	30	xxx
6	vj	50	L
7	vij	51	Lj
8	viij	90	xc
9	jx or ix	100	c
10	x/e	101	cj
11	xj	200	cc
12	xij	1000	m

Fig. 9A

2) Recognizing Whole Words

After a good deal of alphabet practice, you should be ready to begin 'decoding' whole words. This is actually more difficult than to read whole sentences, because a sentence will usually furnish you with contextual clues. In Fig. 9B are individual words from the 17th century documents you will be reading later on. You may refer back to your practice alphabets the first time only. Later, try the section again without reference help. When you can 'read' the examples naturally, you will be ready to proceed to the next section.

3) Practice In Reading Documents

Plates 1 and 2 are examples of typical documents you will be reading: wills and inventories. Skim them first, to get the broad sense of the document, then go back and make a word-for-word transcription. Keep to the lines used in the original and do not alter spelling or expand contractions. Full transcriptions are given at the end of the chapter.

A Note On Dates

Prior to 1753, New Year's Day was held to be March 25th. Therefore, March 24th, 1642 would have been, according to our present calendar March 24th, 1643 (pushing New Year's Day back to January 1st). Exercise caution, therefore, when dating a document which precedes the 19th century. If necessary, write the modern date in parentheses.

Exercise 2

Change to the modern dating system, if necessary:

   I) April 12, 1672
  II) February 21st, 1578
 III) October 9th, 1706
  IV) January 3rd, 1627
   V) November 11th, 1780

Problem: how could a baby have been baptized on November 21st, 1550 and been buried March 2nd, 1550?

Reading And Interpreting Latin

Latin was the legal and ecclesiastical language of Europe

throughout the Middle Ages and remained dominant until the eighteenth century. Even if you do not intend to engage in medieval research, you may well come across parish registers and wills in Latin.

Many English words are derived from Latin and their meaning can be inferred. For example, the Latin 'obiit' and English 'obituary' have a common root meaning 'death'. Many words have also changed meaning over the cenuries, though, so exercise caution when translating. A comprehensive Latin word list is given in Appendix F.

Notes On Latin Grammar

1) Nouns and adjectives. Nouns can be either:

    masculine: ending in - us (e.g. dominus)
    feminine: ending in - a (e.g. puella)
    neuter: ending in - um (e.g. bellum)

The adjective then 'agrees' with the noun and has the same ending. Example:

    puella bona - a good girl
    dominus bonus - a good lord

Many words can be masculine or feminine - judge by the ending.

'Sobrinus' is a male cousin, 'sobrina' is a female cousin. In the word list this is indicated as 'sobrina/us'.

Some nouns end in other ways, such as -er, -is, or -es. All nouns 'decline', that is, change their ending according to their position in the sentence. Examples:

    Puella videt agricolam.
    The girl sees a farmer. BUT:

    Agricola videt puellam.
    The farmer sees the girl.

In Fig. 9C is a table of the most common endings.

2) Verbs. Latin verbs do not need pronouns such as 'I' or 'we': these pronouns are indicated by the ending of the verb. In the word list, you will find the 'I' form of the verb, as it is

easier to work out the other forms from this. Occasionally pronouns were used for emphasis: ego (I), te (you), nos (we).

Present tense of portare (to carry):

```
I: porto                    we: portamus
you: portas                 you: portatis
he: portat                  they: portant
```

Future: take the infinitive (portare) and drop the 're'. This is your future root.

```
portabo - I will carry      portabimus - we will carry
portabis - you will carry   portabitis - you will carry
portabit - he will carry    portabunt - they will carry
```

Past: take the root (porta) and add the endings.

```
portavi - I carried         portavimus - we carried
portavisti - you carried    portavistis - you carried
portavit - he carried       portaverunt - they carried
```

3) Medieval Spelling. Written Latin, like written English, was not uniform; words were often spelled phonetically. If you cannot translate a word, try to work out alternative spellings. Main substitutions are: j for i, i for e, v for u, s for c.

4) Medieval Dating. The Church's calendar of feasts and saints' days were used in preference to the Roman calendar. So, rather than write February 2nd, a scribe would write 'Candlemas' or one of its Latin names. Appendix F lists most major feast days. If you are flummoxed by an unknown saint, refer to the Catholic Encyclopedia.

5) Numerals. Words for numbers are included in Appendix F. Numbers were written thus:

```
    j  1      vij  7      xx  20      xc  90
   ij  2     viij  8     xxx  30       c  100
  iij  3       ix  9      xl  40      cm  900
   iv  4        x  10      l  50       m  1000
    v  5       xj  11     lx  60
   vi  6      xij  12     xc  90
```

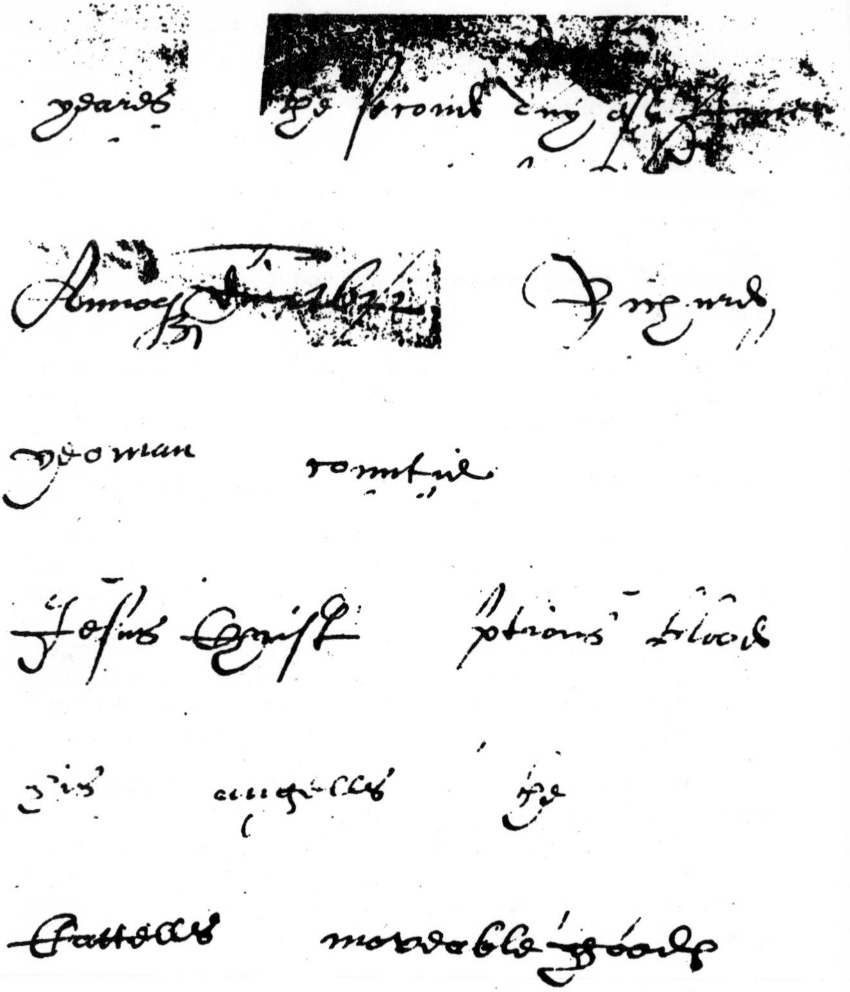

Fig. 9B

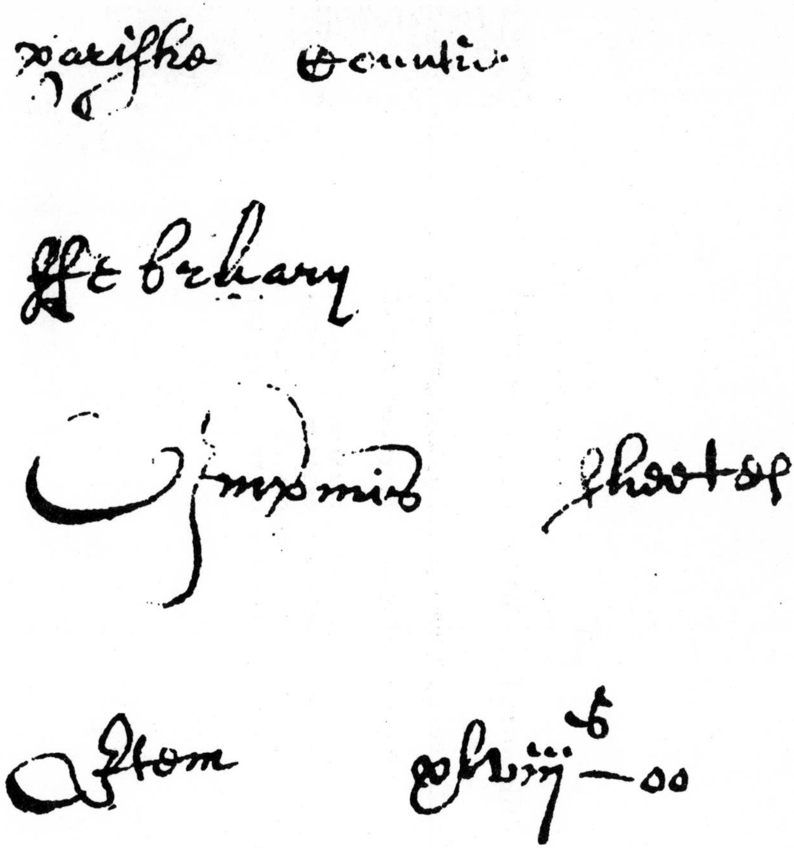

Fig. 9B

Fig. 9C TABLE OF THE MOST COMMON NOUN ENDINGS

	Masculine noun		Feminine noun		Neuter noun	
	Singular	Plural	Singular	Plural	Singular	Plural
Subject	dominus	domini	puella	puellae	castrum	castra
Object	dominum	dominos	puellam	puellas	castrum	castra
'of the'	domini	dominorum	puellae	puellarum	castri	castrorum
'to the'	domino	dominis	puellae	puellis	castro	castris

A true Inventary of the goodes of Roger Workman late of Woodrote in the parishe of Bromsgrove in the Countie of Worcester and ... apprayzed by ... the ... under named the fifth day of ffebruary Anno Domini 1642: Annoq ...... in manner ffollowinge vizt

Imprimis his wearinge apparrell and money in his purse the summe of .... xxₓₓ
Item in the ... nine sheetes one table clothe halfe dozen of table napkins a ... cuppe and salt three ... of pewter at the summe of .... xxₓₓ - 00
Item in the greate barne in corne hay and straw att the summe of .... xxₓₓ - 00
Item in the littill barne hay att the summe of xviij - 00
Item corne growinge in a peece of land called the lyttell ... aikers att the summe of .... xxₓₓ - 00
Item thinges that may be forgotten and not aprayzed - 00 - vjₓ

                          Suma totius - ... xxx ....

The apprayzers
Robert Swylile
Thomas Haightinge
John Chettworth

PLATE 1

PLATE 2

Answers To Exercises In This Chapter

Exercise 1A:
   a) Item one linen cloth
   b) Item one diaper napkin
   c) Item one basin
   d) Item one service book
   e) Item one surplice, for the parson

Exercise 1B:
a) Elizabeth Smith wife of John was buried the 12 of March.
b) Anne born of a wayfaring woman was christened the 20th of March.
c) Jane Waggett wife of Thomas was buried the 26 day of November.
d) William Dunthome and Mary Hunt were married the 20 of April.

Fig. 9B

I)	yeare	XI)	the
II)	second day of June	XII)	chattelles
III)	Anno Domini 1622	XIII)	movable goods
IV)	Richard	XIV)	parishe
V)	yeoman	XV)	countie
VI)	countie	XVI)	February
VII)	Jesus Christ	XVII)	Imprimis
VIII)	precious blood	XVIII)	sheetes
IX)	his	XX)	item
X)	angelles	XXI)	XXVIIIs - ØØ

Plate 1

A true inventory of ye goodes of Roger Wakeman late of Woodcote in the parishe of Bromsgrove in the countie of Worcestershire deceased, apraysed by the prices under named the sixth day of this ffebruary Ann^o Domi 1642: xviii^{th} in manner ffollowinge

	S	D
Imprimis his warminge apparell and money in his purse the sume of	xx	oo
Itm in the ~ler nine sheetes one table cloth halfe duzen of table napkines		

99

a pewter cuppe and three
small pieces of pewter at the
sume of   xx   oo
Item in the greate barne in
corn and hay and strawe att
the sume of   xx   oo
Item in the littell barne
haye att the sume of   xviii   oo
Item corne growinge in
a/ cell of land
called the lyttell wheate
leasowe at the sume of   xx   oo
Item things that maybe for
gotten and not ap aysed   oo   vj_d

suma   vi^h   viij^s   vj

The ap^r aysers
Robert Wylde
Thomas ffaighting
John Chellingworth

1. parlour
2. a parcel

Plate 2

(In the name of) God Amen the second day of June in the
yeare of the raigne of O^r sovreign Lord James the grace of
God of England, France, and Ireland King defender of the faith
... the twentieth and of Scotland the five and fortieth Anno
Dmi 1622.   I Richard Hall of Chadwich yeeld (thelder?) in the
prshe of Bromsgrove in the countie of Worcester yeoman
weake in bodie but stronge in mynde do willingly and wth a full
heart remer and give againe into the hands of my Lord God
and creat^r my spirite wch he of his fatherly goodness gave
unto me nothing doubting but that for his infinite mercies ....
in the pcious blood of his dearly beloved sonne Jesus Christ
O^r only savior and redeemer he will receave my soule into his
glorie and place it in the companie of heavenly angelles and
blessed Sainte Ann and commending it to the earth whereof it
came nothing doubting but trusting to the...of my faith and the
great day of the generall Resurrection when we shall all ap-
peare before the iudgement seate of Christ and shall receave
the same againe by the mightie power of God not a corruptible
mortall weake and sicke bodie as it is now but   an incorrup-
tible immortall stronge and pfect bodie in all points like unto

100

the glorious bodie of my Lord and Saviour Jesus Christ.

1. parish
2. precious

Exercise 2
I)	April 12th 1672
II)	February 21st, 1579
III)	October 9th, 1706
IV)	January 3rd, 1628
V)	November 11th, 1780

The baby was baptized in November 1550. In January, we begin dating 1551 but people then figured 1551 to begin on March 25th. Therefore March 2nd would have been written as 1550.

EPILOGUE

Tracing your genealogy and family history is a fascinating past-time and I hope that the reader will find the guidance in this book both informative encouraging. The fabric of history has been woven by millions of individuals and their lives deserve to be recorded. Many left evidence of their movements and actions in censuses, parish registers, vestry minutes, and poll, even if they themselves were illiterate. It is our task to unearth this evidence and place it in logical sequence.

It is my hope that the section on archaic script and language will not disconcert but will leave you with a feeling of accomplishment at mastering virtually a new language. If you wish to learn more about paleography, please refer to the bibliography.

The hints for traveling genealogists have been a result of my own experiences and I sincerely hope that they aid you in planning and implementing a successful research trip. Enjoy your visit to the old country - may it be fruitful and happy!

BIBLIOGRAPHY

Burke, A.M. *Key To The Ancient Parish Reg-isters.* London, 1908.

Cox, Jane and Padfield, Timothy. *Tracing Your Ancestors In The Public Record Office.* London: Her Majesty's Stationery Office, 1981.

Emmison, F.G. *Archives And Local History.* London: Methuen, 1966.

Emmison, F.G. *How To Read Local Archives 1550-1700.* London: Historical Association, 1967.

Gardner, D.E. et al. *Genealogical Research In England And Wales.* Salt Lake City, UT: Book-craft, 1956-1959.

Grieve, Hilda. *Examples Of English Handwriting 1150-1750.* Essex Record Office, 1966.

West, John. *Village Records.* London: Phillimore, 1962, 1982.

Tate, W.E. *The Parish Chest.* Cambridge University Press, 1960.

APPENDIX A

COUNTY AND LOCAL RECORD OFFICES

* denotes Saturday hours; inquire for particulars

Bedfordshire
Bedfordshire County Record Office, County Hall, Bedford MK42 9AP; tel: Bedford 63222 ext. 277

Berkshire
Berkshire Record Office, Shire Hall, Reading, Berkshire RG1 3EE; tel: Reading 55981

Bristol see Gloucestershire

Birmingham see West Midlands

Buckinghamshire
Buckinghamshire Record Office, County Hall, Aylesbury, Buckinghamshire HP20 1VA; tel: Aylesbury 5000

Cambridgeshire
Cambridge County Record Office, Shire Hall, Cambridge CB1 0AP; tel: Cambridge 58811 ext 281

Cambridge University Archives, West Road, Cambridge CB3 9DR

Wisbech and Fenland Museum, Museum Square, Wisbech, Cambridgeshire; tel: 0945-583817

Cheshire
Cheshire Record Office*, The Castle, Chester CH1 2DN; tel: 061 480 2966

Cornwall
Cornwall County Record Office*, County Hall, Truro, Cornwall TR1 3AY; tel: Truro 74282

Cumberland
Cumbria County Record Office, The Castle, Carlisle CA3 8UR; tel: Carlisle 23456 ext 316

Derbyshire
Derbyshire Record Office*, County Offices, Matlock, Derbyshire DE4 3AG; tel: Derbyshire (continued)
Matlock 3411

Devon
Devon County Record Office, Castle Street, Exeter EX4 3BQ; tel: Exeter 79146

Devon Record Office (for West Devon), 14, Tavistock Place, Plymouth, Devon PL4 8AN; tel: Plymouth 28293

Dorset
Dorset County Record Office, County Hall, Dorchester, Dorset DT1 1XJ; tel: Dorchester 3131

Durham
Durham County Record Office, County Hall, Durham DH1 5UL; tel: Durham 64411

Darlington Public Library, Crown Street, Darlington DL1 1ND; tel: Darlington 69858

Essex
Essex Record Office, County Hall, Chelmsford, Essex CM1 1LX; tel: Chelmsford 67222

Gloucestershire
Gloucestershire County Record Office, Worcester St., Gloucester GL1 3DW; tel: Gloucester 21444 ext 229

Bristol City Record Office*, The Council House, College Green, Bristol BS1 5TR; tel: Bristol 26031 ext 442

Hampshire
Hampshire Record Office, 20 Southgate Street, Winchester, Hampshire SO23 9EF; tel: Winchester 63153

Portsmouth City Record Office, The Guildhall, Portsmouth, Hampshire PO1 2AL; tel: Portsmouth 21771

Southampton Civic Record Office, Civic Centre, Southampton SO9 4XL; tel: Southampton 23855

Hereford
Hereford Record Office, The Old Barracks, Harold Street, Hereford HR1 2QX; tel: Hereford 65441

Hertfordshire
Hertfordshire Record Office, County Hall, Room 200 Library Block, Hartford SG13 8DE; tel: Hertford 54242

Humberside see Lincolnshire and Yorkshire

Huntingdonshire
Huntingdonshire County Record Office, Grammar School Walk, Huntingdon PE18 6LF; tel: Huntingdon 52181

Kent
Kent Archives Office, County Hall, Maidstone, Kent ME11 1XH; tel: Maidstone 67411 ext 3312

Cathedral Archives and Library, The Precincts, Canterbury, Kent CT1 2EG; tel: Canterbury 63510

Diocesan Registry, The Precincts, Rochester, Kent; tel: Medway 4323

Institute of Heraldic and Genealogical Studies, Northgate, Canterbury, Kent; tel: Canterbury 68664

Lancashire
Lancashire County Record Office, Bow Lane, Preston, Lancashire PR1 8ND; tel: Preston 51905

Archives Department, Manchester Public Libraries, Central Library, St. Peter's Square, Manchester M2 5PD; tel: Manchester 236 7401

Liverpool Record Office*, Brown Picton and Homly Libraries, William Brown St., Liverpool L3 8EW; tel: Liverpool 207 2147

Leicestershire
Leicestershire Record Office, 57, New Walk, Leicester LE1 7JB; tel: Leicester 539111

Lincolnshire
Lincolnshire Record Office, The Castle, Lincoln LN1 3AB; tel: Lincoln 25158

South Humberside Area Record Office*, Central Library, Town Hall Square, Grimsby, S. Humberside DN31 1HG; tel: Grimsby 59161 ext. 253

London and Middlesex Greater London Record Office, The County Hall, London SE1 7PB; tel: 01 633 8186 or 7808

Middlesex County Records: Greater London Record Office, 1, Queen Anne's Gate Buildings, Dartmouth Street, London SW1Y 9BS

Corporation of London Records: Guildhall, London EC2P 2EJ; tel: 01 606 3030

Lambeth Palace Library, London SE1 7JU

Norfolk
Norfolk Record Office*, Central Library, Norwich NR2 1NJ; tel: Norwich 22211 ext 599

see also Cambridgeshire Wisbech and Fenland Museum

Northamptonshire
Northamptonshire Record Office and Southwell Diocesan Record Office*, County House, High Pavement, Nottingham NG1 1HR; tel: Nottingham 54524

Oxfordshire
Oxfordshire County Record Office, County Hall, New Road, Oxford OX1 1ND; tel: Oxford 49861

Bodleian Library, Oxford OX1 3BG; tel: Oxford 44675

Oxford Central Library, Westgate, Oxford; tel: Oxford 722422

Rutland see Leicestershire

Shropshire

Shropshire County Record Office, The Shirehall, Abbey Foregate, Shrewsbury SY2 6ND; tel: Shrewsbury 222406

Somerset

Somerset County Record Of-fice*, Obridge Road, Taunton, Somerset TA2 7PU; tel: Taunton 87600

Bath City Record Office, The Guildhall, Bath BA4 5AW; tel: Bath 28411 ext 201

Staffordshire

Staffordshire County Record Office, County Buildings, Eastgate Street, Stafford ST16 2LZ; tel: Stafford 3121 ext 7923

Lichfield Joint Record Office, Lichfield Library, Bird Street, Lichfield WS13 6PN; tel: Lichfield 56787

Suffolk

East – Suffolk County Record Office*, County Hall, Ipswich IP4 2JS; tel: Ipswich 55801

West – Suffolk County Record Office*, Schoolhall Street, Bury St. Edmunds IP33 1RX; tel: Bury St. Edmunds 63141

Surrey

Surrey County Record Office, County Hall, Kingston-upon-Thames, Surrey KT1 2DN; tel: 01 546 1050 ext 3561

Sussex

East Sussex County Records Office, Pelham House, St. Andrew's Lane, Lewes, East Sussex BN7 1UN; tel: Lewes 5400

West Sussex County Record Office and Chichester Diocesan Record Office, County Hall, Chichester, West Sussex PO19 1RN; tel: Chi-chester 85100 ext 351

Warwickshire

Warwickshire County Record Office*, Priory Park, Cape Road, Warwick CV34 4JS; tel: Warwick 493431 ext 2508

Coventry City Record Office, 9, Hay Lane, Coventry CV1 5RF

West Midlands
Birmingham Reference Library, Central Library, Paradise Circus, Queensway, Birmingham; tel: 021 235 3591

Westmoreland
Westmoreland County Record Office, Council Offices, Kendal, Cumbria; tel: Kendal 21000

Isle of Wight
Isle of Wight County and Diocesan Record Office, 26, Hillside, Newport, Isle of Wight PO30 3EB; tel: Newport 4031 ext 32

Wiltshire
Wiltshire County Record Office, County Hall, Trowbridge, Wiltshire; tel: Trowbridge 3641 ext 3502

Diocesan Record Office, The Wren Hall, The Close, Salisbury, Wiltshire; tel: Salisbury 22519

Worcestershire
Worcestershire County Record Office, Shire Hall, Worcester; tel: Worcester 23400 ext 118

Yorkshire
North Yorkshire County Record Office, County Hall, Northallerton, North Yorkshire DL7 8SG; tel: Northallerton 3123 ext 455

West Yorkshire County Record Office, County Hall, Wakefield WF1 2QW; tel: Wakefield 67111 ext 2352

South Yorkshire County Record Office, Ellin Street, Sheffield S1 4PL; tel: Sheffield 2919 ext 33

Borthwick Institute of Historical Research, Peasholme Green, York YO1 2PV

Humberside County Record Office, County Hall, Beverly, N. Humberside; tel: Beverly 887131

Kingston–upon–Hull Record Office, Guildhall, Kingston–upon–Hull, N Humberside HU1 2AA; tel: Kingston–Upon–Hull 223111 ext 407

APPENDIX B

DENOMINATIONAL REPOSITORIES

Nonconformists in general:

Dr. William's Library, 14, Gordon Square, London WC1H 0AG; tel: 01 387 1310

Specific nonconformist denominations:

United Reformed Church History Society, 86, Tavistock Place, London WC1; tel: 01 837 7661

Congregational Library, Memorial Hall, Farringdon Street, London EC4; tel: 01 236 2223

Baptist Union Library, 4, Southampton Row, London WC1; tel: 01 405 9803

Society of Friends Library, Friends House, Euston Road, London NW1; tel: 01 387 3601

Methodist Archives, Division of Property, Central Buildings, Oldham Street, Manchester M1 1JQ

Roman Catholicism

Catholic Record Society, 114, Mount Street, London W1Y 6AH
Jewish Records

Jewish Museum, Woburn House, Upper Woburn Place, London WC1; tel 01 387 3081/2

APPENDIX C

MEMBERS OF THE FEDERATION OF FAMILY HISTORY SOCIETIES IN GREAT BRITAIN AND THE UNITED STATES

Society of Genealogists
Mr. A. J. Camp, 14, Charterhouse Buildings, Goswell Road, London EC1M 7BA

Institute of Heraldic and Genealogical Studies
Miss S. Fincher, Northgate, Canterbury, Kent

Avon see Bristol and Avon

Bedfordshire FHS
Mr. C. West, 17, Lombard St, Lidlington, Bedford MK43 0RP

Berkshire FHS
Mr. J. Gurnett, 34, Hawkesbury Drive, Fords Farm, Calcot, Reading, Berkshire RG3 5ZR

Birmingham & Midland Society for Genealogy & Heraldry
Mrs. J. Watkins, 92 Dimmingsdale Bank, Birmingham, West Midlands B32 1ST

Bristol and Avon FHS
Mrs. K. Kearsey, 135, Cotham Brown, Bristol BS6 6AD

Buckinghamshire FHS
Mrs. E. McLaughlin, 18 Rudds Lane, Haddenham, Aylesbury, Bucks.

Cambridgeshire FHS
Mrs. P. Close, 56 The Street, Kirtling, Newmarket, Cambridgeshire CB8 9PB

FHS of Cheshire
Mrs. D. Foxcroft, 5 Gordon Ave., Bromborough, Wirral, Merseyside

Cleveland FHS
Mr. A. Sampson, 1, Oxgang Close, Redcar TS10 4ND

Cornwall FHS
Mr. M. Martin, Chimneypots, Sunny Corner, Cusgarne, Truro, Cornwall TR4 8SE

Cumbria FHS
Mrs. M. Russell, 32 Granada Road, Denton, Manchester M34 2LJ

Derbyshire FHS
Mrs. P. Marples, 15, Elmhurst Road, Forest Town, Mansfield, Nottinghamshire NG19 0EV

Devon FHS
Miss V. Bluett, 63, Old Laira Road, Laira, Plymouth, Devon PL3 5BL

Doncaster FHS
Miss E. Whitehouse, 7 Sherburn Close, Skellow, Doncaster, S. Yorkshire DN 6 8LG

Dorset see **Somerset & Dorset**

Durham see **Northumberland & Durham**

Essex FHS
Mr. C. Lewis, 48, Walton Road, Frinton-on-Sea, Essex CO13 0AG

Folkestone & District
Mrs. M. Criddle, 22, Church Road, Cheriton, Folkestone, Kent

Gloucestershire FHS
Mr. J. Vaughan, 1, Roxton Drive, The Reddings, Cheltenham, Glos. GL51 6SQ

Hampshire Genealogical Society
Mrs. J. Hobbs, 12, Ashling House, Chidham Walk, Havant, Hants. PO9 1DY

Herefordshire FHS
Mrs. V. Hadley, 255, Whitecross Road, Hereford HR4 0LT

Hertfordshire F&PHS
Mrs. J. Laidlaw, 155, Jessop Road, Stevenage, Herts.

Kent FHS
Mrs. H. Lewis, 17, Abbots Place, Canterbury, Kent CT1 2AH

North West Kent FHS
Miss J. M. Biggs, 39, Nightingale Road, Petts Wood, Orping-
ton, Kent BR5 1BH

Lancashire Family History and Heraldry Society
Mr. R. Hampson, 7, Margaret Street, Oldham, Lancs. OL2
8RP

Leicestershire FHS
Miss S. Brown, 25, Homecroft Drive, Packington, Ashby de la
Zouche, Leics.

Society for Lincolnshire History & Arch. (Family History
Section)
Mrs. E Robson, 135 Baldertongate, Newark, Notts. NG24 1RY

Liverpool & District FHS
Mr. H. Culling, 11, Lisburn Lane, Tuebrook, Liverpool

East of London FHS
Mr. A. Polybank, Flat 2, 193-7 Mile End Road, London E1
4AA

Isle of Man FHS
Miss P. Killip, 9, Sandringham Drive, Onchan, IOM

Manchester & Lancashire FHS
Mr. E. Crosby, 32, Bournlea Avenue, Burnage, Manchester
M19 1AF

Central Middlesex FHS
Mrs E. V. Pirie, 44, Dorchester Avenue, North Harrow, Middlesex HA2 7AU

North Middlesex FHS
Miss J. Lewis, 15, Milton Road, Walthamstow, London E17

West Middlesex FHS
Mrs. M. Morton, 92, Avondale Ave, Staines, Middlesex TW18 2NF

Norfolk & Norwich GS
Miss C. Hood, 293, Dereham Road, Norwich NR2 3TH

Northamtonshire FHS
Miss L. Wesley, 56, Gloucester Crescent, Delapre, Northampton NN4 9PR

Northumberland & Durham FHS
Mr. J. K. Brown, 33, South Bend, Brunton Park, Newcastle-on-Tyne, NE3 5TR

Nottinghamshire FHS
Miss S. M. Leeds, 35, Kingswood Road, West Bridgford, Nottingham NG2 7HT

Oxfordshire FHS
Mrs. V. Lee, Speedwell, North Moreton, Oxon. OX11 9BG

Peterborough & District FHS
Mrs. C. Newman, 106, London Road, Peterborough, Cambs PE2 9BY

Sheffield & District FHS
Mrs. E. Furey, 58, Stumperlowe Crescent Road, Sheffield, S10 3PR

Shropshire FHS
Mrs. G. Lewis, 15, Wesley Drive, Oakengates, Telford, Shropshire TF2 0DZ

Somerset & Dorset FHS
Mr. T. P. Farmer, BruLands, Marston Road, Sherborne, Dorset DT9 4BL

Staffordshire see Birmingham

Suffolk Genealogy Society
Mrs. K. Bardwell, 2, Fern Avenue, North Oulton Broad, Lowestoft, Suffolk

East Surrey FHS
Mrs. M. Brackpool, 370, Chipstead Valley Road, Coulsdon, Surrey CR3 3BF

West Surrey FHS
Mrs. M. Taylor, 60, Ashley Road, Farnborough, Hants. GU14 7HB

Sussex FHS
Mrs. B. Mottershead, 44 The Green, Southwick, Sussex, BN4 4FR

Waltham Forest FHS
Mrs. J. Thompson, 49 Tavistock Avenue, Walthamstow, London E17 6HR

Warwickshire see **Birmingham**

Wiltshire FHS
Mrs. M. R. Moore, 17, Blakeney Avenue, Nythe, Swindon, Wilts. SN3 3NE

Windsor, Slough & District FHS
Mrs. J. Catlin, 2, Faircroft, Slough SL2 1HJ, Bucks.

Woolwich & District FHS
Ms. S. Highley, 4, Church Road, Bexleyheath, Kent

Worcestershire see **Birmingham**

Yorks. Arch. Society (Family and Pop. Studies Section)
Mrs. B. Shimwell, 24, Holt Park Road, Adel, Leeds LS16 7QS

East Yorks. FHS
Mr. R. E. Walgate, 9 Stepney Grove, Scarborough, North Yorks. YO12 5DF

York FHS
Mrs. F. Foster, 1, Ouse Lea, Shipton Road, York YO3 6SA

****

International Society for British Genealogy and Family History
POB 20425, Cleveland OH 44120

National Genealogical Society
4527 17th St N., Arlington VA 22207-2363

Chicago Genealogical Society
POB 1160, Chicago IL 60690

Florida Genealogical Society
POB 18624, Tampa FL 33679

International Genealogy Fellowship of Rotarians
5721 Antietam Dr., Sarasota FL 33581

Ventura County Genealogical Society
POB DN, Ventura CA 93002

Houston Genealogical Forum
POB 271469, Houston TX 77277-1469

Jefferson County Genealogical Society
POB 174, Oskaloosa KS 66066

English Interest Group, Minnesota Genealogical Society
9009 Northwood Circle, New Hope MN 55427

Santa Barbara County Genealogical Society
POB 1174, Goleta CA 93116

Genealogical Association of Sacramento
1230 42nd Ave., Sacramento CA 95822

Utah Genealogical Society
POB 1144, Salt Lake City UT 84110

Seattle Genealogical Society
POB 549, Seattle WA 98111

APPENDIX D

REGIONAL TOURIST BOARDS OF ENGLAND

London
British Tourist Authority Information Center, 64 St. James's Street, London SW1; tel: 01-499-9325

London Tourist Board, 26 Grosvenor Gardens, London SW1; tel: 01-730 0791

NOTE: For personal callers only, the L.T.B. has bureaux on Platform 15 at Victoria Station, Harrods Fourth Floor, Selfridges Ground Floor and Heathrow Central Underground Station..

South East England Tourist Board
Chevoit House, 4-6 Monson Road, Tunbridge Wells, Kent; tel: 0892 40766

Southern Tourist Board
Old Town Hall, Leigh Road, Eastleigh, Hampshire; tel: 0703 616027

Isle of Wight Tourist Board
21 High Street, Newport, Isle of Wight; tel: 0983 524343 or 525141

West Country Tourist Board
Trinity Court, 37 Southernhay East, Exeter, Devon; tel: 0392 76351

West Midlands
Heart of England Tourist Board, POB 15, Worcester; tel: 0905 29511

South Midlands
Thames and Chilterns Tourist Board, POB 10, 8 The Market Place, Abingdon, Oxon.; tel: 0235 22711

East Anglia Tourist Board
14 Museum Street, Ipswich, Suffolk; tel: 0473 214211

East Midlands Tourist Board
Exchequergate, Lincoln; tel: 0522 31521

Lancashire, Cheshire & Peak District
North West Tourist Board, The Last Drop Village, Bromley Cross, Bolton, Lancashire; tel: 0204 591511

Yorkshire & Humberside Tourist Board
312 Tadcaster Road, York, North Yorkshire; tel: 0904 707961

Isle of Man Tourist Board
13 Victoria Street, Douglas, Isle of Man; tel: 0624 4323

Cumbria, Northumbria & Durham
Northumbria Tourist Board, 9 Osborne Terrace, Newcastle-upon-Tyne; tel: 0632 817744

British Tourist Authority Offices in the USA
680 5th Ave., New York NY 10019; tel: (212) 581-4700

612 S Flower St., Los Angeles CA 90017; tel: (213) 623 8196

John Hancock Center, 875 N. Michigan Ave. #3320, Chicago IL 60611; tel: (312)-787- 0490

These offices can supply general information, maps, etc.

APPENDIX E

AMERICAN/ENGLISH VOCABULARY LIST

AMERICAN	ENGLISH
baggageroom	left luggage office
band-aid	elastoplast/plaster
bathtub	bath
billfold	wallet
broil	grill
call collect	reverse charges
carnival	fair
check (restaurant)	bill
chips	crisps
closet	wardrobe
dessert	pudding/sweet
divided hwy	dual carriageway
down town	city centre
druggist	chemist
elevator	lift
fall	autumn
faucet	tap
freeway	motorway
French fries	chips
garbage can	dustbin
directory assistance	directory enquiries
janitor	caretaker
lawyer	solicitor
legal holiday	bank holiday
liquor	spirits
long distance	trunk call
lost & found	lost property
mailbox	pillar box
make reservation	book
movie theater	cinema

news dealer	newsagent
odometer	mileometer
one way ticket	single ticket
outlet/socket	power point
pantie hose	tights
parking lot	car park
pass (vehicle)	overtake
pavement	road
period	full-stop
pullman	sleeping-car
purse/pocket book	handbag
raincoat	mac/macintosh
restroom	cloakroom/toilet or lavatory
round trip ticket	return ticket
salesclerk	shop-assistant
schedule	timetable
sidewalk	pavement
stand in line	queue
stoplight	traffic light
two weeks	fortnight
windshield	windscreen
wire	telegram
with or without milk/cream	black or white?
yard	garden
zero	nought
zip code	postal code

APPENDIX F

MEDIEVAL LATIN WORD LIST

abatio	annulment
abavia/us	2nd great-grandmother/ father
abortivus	prematurely born
accasatus	resident tenant
acuarius	needlemaker
addico	I promise
adolescens	young man
adoperatio	working; application
adoptivus	adopted
adprimas	first of all
adultus	young boy
aedilis	architect
aetas	age
aetatis	aged
agellarius	husbandman
agenda	mass for the dead
agnomentum	surname
agricola	farmer
aldermannus	ealdorman, nobleman
alius	the other (of 2)
alleluia clausum	Septuagissima Sunday
alutarius	both (of this parish)
amicus	kinsman
amita	aunt on father's side
amita magna	grandfather's sister
androchia	dairymaid
anella	old woman
anime	masses for the dead
Animarum commemoratio	All Soul's Day (Nov. 2)
anno domini	in the year of our Lord

annonymus/a	stillborn child
Annuntiatio	the Annunciatio (March 25)
apothecarius	pharmacist
apprenticius	apprentice
approbatio testamenti	probate of testament
archiator	doctor
arcularius	carpenter
argentum	cash
armentarius	herdsman
asarcha	Lent
Assumptio	Feast of the Assumption (Aug. 15)
Assumptio a Salvatoris Day	Ascension Day
atava	grandmother
aucarius	gooseherd
aurifaber	goldsmith
avia	grandmother
avuncula	aunt
ava/us	grandmother/father
avunculus magnus/major	great-uncle
baccalaureus	bachelor
ballistrarius	gunsmith
baptizatio	baptism
barcarius	shipmaker
bastardus	bastard
beda	prayer
belmannus	bell-ringer
bercarius	shepherd, tanner
bidens	sheep
bigamia	2nd marriage
bijuges (pl.)	candelaria
bolstera	bolster
bondus	head of household
boverius	oxherd
bovicula	heifer
boviculus	bullock
bostio	plough-boy
bramum	well, pit
Brandones	1st Sunday in Lent
braciator	brewer
bubularius	oxherd
bubulcus	oxherd, ploughman
buscarius	butcher
butularius	butter

buttarius	cooper
buistarius	box-maker
chivalerus	knight
cabo	stallion
caelebs	see celebs
caligator	hosier
camera	room, chamber
campana	bell, clock
campanitor	bell-ringer
campus	field
campester	peasant
Candelaria	Candlemas (February 2nd)
candelifex	chandler
capa	cape, hooded cloak
carbo	coal
carbonarius	coal-miner
carecarius	carter, ploughman
caretta	cart
carnificium	shambles, meat market
carnlevaria	Shrove Tuesday
carnisbrevium	beginning of Lent
carrucator	ploughman
casale	village
caskettum	casket
cassatio	nullification
catabulum	pigsty
catallum & capitale	chattel, moveable goods
Cathedra, Festum Sancti Petri in,	St. Peter's Chair (Feb. 22)
causarius	hatmaker
celebs	single or widowed
cellarium	store-room
cellarius	butler
cimiterius	mason
(dies) cene ad mandatum	Maundy Thursday
cerefactor	chandler
cervisiarius	ale-house keeper
Charisma	Whit Sunday
chirothecator	glover
chirugus	surgeon
Circumcisio Domini	The Circumcision (Jan. 1)
cista	coffin
cistarius	box-maker
cistator	treasurer
Clausio Pasche	Sunday after Easter
Clausio Pentecostes	Trinity Sunday

claustrarius	locksmith
coffinarius	basket-maker
cognatus	cousin, kinsman
comes	earl, count
commater	godmother
compater	godfather
Conceptio Beati Virginis	Feast of the Conception (December 8)
conjug:	married
connutrucius	foster-brother
contractio	marriage contract
Conversatio Sancti Pauli	Conversion of St. Paul (Jan. 25)
convicina	neighbor
coppa	hen
coquina	kitchen furniture
cordifer	rope-maker
cordonarius	leather-maker
(festum dies) corpus Christi	Thursday after Trinity
cotuca	tunic
cotarius	cottager
crastinum	tomorrow
croftum	plot of land
crumenarius	pursemaker
cudarus	forester
cutellarius	cutler
cum	by, with
coupa	cup, bowl
cupbordum	cupboard
cutissima	curtain
custor	sacristan
d.s.p.	died without issue
d.v.m.	died while mother living
d.v.p.	died while father living
dayaria	dairy
decada	ten
decennarius	tithing-man
decima	tithing
(festum) Decollationis Sancti Johanni Baptisti	Beheading of St. John (Aug 29)
deducator ferarum	gamekeeper
defensiva	fence
denarius	penny
derelicta	widow
desponsatio	betrothal, marriage
didymus	twin

dies Dominica	Sunday
dies Soles	Sunday
dies Lune	Monday
dies Martis	Tuesday
dies Mercurii	Wednesday
dies Wodenis	Wednesday
dies Jovis	Thursday
dies Veneris	Friday
dies Veneris Bonus/Sancta	Good Friday
dies Sabbati (-nus)	Saturday
dies Saturni	Saturday
digamus	twice married
disjugata	unmarried woman
dispunctuo	settle accounts
deviso	bequeath
doga	wainscot
domesticalia	household goods
domus	house
domus brasinea	brew-house
domus carbonum	coal-house
domus cervisiana	ale-house
domus feni	barn
domus porcorum	pigsty
domus vaccarum	cow-shed
domificator	carpenter, builder
dos	dower, endowment
drapa	cloth
draperus	draper
dressura	serving-board
ducena	twelve
dum	when, since
eductio carruce	Plough Monday (1st after Epiphany)
eloco	give in marriage
emptum	purchase
engia (pl)	mortgage
enopola	taverner
entalliator	stone-carver
ephestris	surcoat
ephipparius	saddler
Epiphania Domini	Epiphany (Jan 6)
equus	horse
eques	knight
ergo	therefore
ericetum	heath, moor
eruptio	spring of water

129

escaria	sideboard
escarium	manger
et	and
(festum) exaltionis Sancti Crucis	Holy Cross Day (Sept. 14)
excusor	printer
executor testamenti	executor of will
exheredatus	disinherited
exlex	outlaw
expensa	storeroom
extravagus	vagrant
faber cupri	coopersmith
faber ferrarius	blacksmith
faber lignarius	joiner
faber scriniarius	cabinet-maker
fabrica	forge
falcata	measure of a meadow
famulia	household
fantulus/fantula	little boy or girl
fenestra	window
fena	hay-fields
ferdingus	farthing (1/4 penny)
feria	festival, weekday
feria prima	Sunday
feria secunda etc.	Monday
ferma	farm
ferocia	quilt, mattress
ferreum	horse-shoe
ferrifaber	iron-smith
fidatio	betrothal
fidejussor	godparent
filius	son
filius in lege	son-in-law
filius naturalis	bastard
filiaster	stepson, son-in-law
filiastra	step-daughter
filiola/us	god-daughter/son
fiscalia	taxes
flecciator	fletcher
florinus	gold coin
focarium	hearth
fons	well
foramen	window-pane
fossor	digger, miner

130

fotherator	furrier
frater	brother
frater in lege	brother-in-law
fratruelusa/us	niece/nephew
frethum	hedge
fritha	woodland, pasture
frumentum	wheat
frunitor	tanner
fugarius	drover
fullaticus	fuller
furlongus	furlong (1/8 mile)
Galilea	porch of church
galitarius	shoemaker
ganata	bowl
garba	sheaf (of corn)
garcifer	servant
gardinum	garden, orchard
gardinarius	gardener
gavella	family holding
geldum	tax
gemelli	twins
gilda	guild
(terra) glebalis	glebe-land
grabatum	skirt
gramen	pasturage
grammaticulus	schoolboy
grana	grain
granarium	granary
grangia decimalis	tithe-barn
grotus	groat (coin)
habedassarius	haberdasher
hebdomada	week
heres	heir
histrio	player, minstrel
homo	man
hordeum	barley
horilogium	clock
horrea	barn
hortus	garden
hortulanus	gardener
hospitium	household
hostillarius	inn-keeper
humatus	buried
hundredum	hundred (division of county)
husbandus	husbandman

hypante	Candlemas (Feb. 2)
ignotus	illegitimate
imbrevio	to record in writing
impendo	give, spend
impraegnata	pregnant before marriage
imprimis	in the first place
inconjugatus	unwed
indigentia (pl)	necessaries
infrascriptus	written below
inhumatio	burial
(festum) innocentium	Holy Innocents (Dec. 28)
insinuo	register a will
intratio	entry (into a building)
ire (eo)	go
itaquod	on condition that
iter	path
item	next (on list), also
jakkum	sleeveless tunic
jejunium guadragesimale	Lent
(caput) jejuni	Ash Wednesday
judex	judge
juramentus exhibitum fuit	certificate (of burial in wool)
jus	right, due
juvencula	girl
juvenis	young man
juxta	according to
laboratio	ploughing
laboro ad	work at
laicus	layman
lana	wool or wool-tax
lanatus	"buried in wool"
lanifex	clothier
landa	untilled land
lapis	stone (weight)
lararium	closet
lardaria	larder
largitas	width
latro	thief
lautumus	mason
lectus	bed-clothes, bed
legatio	legacy
lego in manus	bequeath
laetare	third Sunday of Lent
liber	book, freeman
libra	pound (weight or money)

lignarius	joiner
lignum	wood
ligniscissor	woodcutter
linea	linen cloth or garment
macellaria	meat-market
macellarius	butcher
macerio	mason
magister	master (of school or trade)
major	adult
mala	rent, mail
malarium	orchard
malluvium	wash-basin
maunda	hamper
mare	sea
maria	lake
marium	moor, marsh
maritagium	marriage
maritellus	husband
mater	mother
mater meretrix	illegitimate mother
matrimonium	dowry
mauseolum	coffin, tomb
medicus	physician
mensa	food, table
meta	boundary
methodus	road
migratio ad	die
Christum/Dominum miles	knight
mille	thousand
mobile	movable goods
modius	a peck (measure
molendinum	mill
molendinum venti	windmill
molitarius corlii	leather-worker
morganaticus	morganatic (marriage)
multrix	milk-maid
mulier	wife
multardus	shepherd
munimen	enclosure
murena	marsh
murus	wall
napiria	table linen
natalicium	birthday, Saint's day
natalicium Dominicum	Christmas
nativitas	birthplace
nativitatis Domini	Christmas

nativitas beate Marie	Birth of the Blessed Mary (Sept. 8)
nepos	nephew
neptis	niece
netrix	spinster
nomen proprium	baptismal name
novercarius (testamentum)	stepfather
noncupative facto	oral will
nubo	give in marriage
nubo me	wed
obiit	died
obiit sine prole	died without issue
opus	work
orphanus	orphan
ovis	sheep
ovianus	shepherd
pactum	contract, lease
pagus	village
pajettus	page, servant
pallium	funeral shroud
(Dominica) in palmis	Palm Sunday
palus	marsh, fence
pandoxatorium	ale-house
panis	bread
palna	roof-timber storey of house
pannus	cloth, garment
paraphernalia	married woman's property
(dies) paracevensis	Good Friday
parentalia	family, kin
parochia	parish, parish church
Pascha	Easter Sunday
Pascha Album	Low Sunday
Pascha Minus	Palm Sunday
dies Lune Paschalis	Easter Monday
pascua & pastura	pasture
patella	bowl, pan
pater	father
pater in lege	father-in-law
patrinus	godfater
patruus magnus	great-uncle
pauso	rest, die
peciata	peck (measure)
pecunia	money
pelvis	basin
penarium	cupboard

pendilium	curtain
Pentecoste	Pentecost
penulator	furrier
per	by, on (day of the week)
peregrinus	pilgrim
perempticius	apprentice
(dies Luna) perjurata	second Monday after Easter
persinctus	boundary
persolutio	payment in full
pestilentia	the Plague
pictor	painter
pilleus	cap
pincernarius	butler
piscenarius	fishmonger
platula	plate
plus	more
polis	city
polata	pole (measure of land)
pomarium	orchard
pondus	weight, pound
porcarius	swineherd
porcus	pig
posteritas	descendants
purcingtus	boundary
preco	watchman
precontractus	precontract (of marriage)
pregnatus	pregnant
prehibitus	aforesaid
prememoratus	previously mentioned
presbyter	old man, priest
prevolentia	antecedent will
prida	mortgage
primogenitor	first-born
prevignus	stepson
pro	because of, for
proava/us	great-grandmother/father
procreamen	offspring
proles	offspring
proles spuria	illegitimate offspring
propinquitas	kinsfolk
provincia	shire, county
pucella & puella	girl
puer	boy
puerpera	mother
Purificans	Candlemas (February 2)

135

quadragesima	Lent
(Dominica) quadragesime	first Sunday in Lent
quadravus	great-great-grandfather
quadriga	wagon
quasimodo geniti	Low Sunday
quondam	formerly
quoniam	since, because
Ramispalme	Palm Sunday
relicta	widow
(dies Dominica) reliquiarium	Relic Sunday (first after July 7)
resurrectio Dominica	Easter Sunday
roparius	rope-maker
rusticus	peasant
(dies) Sabbatinus	Saturday
(dies) Sabbatainus sanctus	Holy Saturday
sacerdos	priest
sarrator	sawyer
shamellum	shambles, meat market
shira	shire
scholarius	scholar
scilicet	namely
scotus de capite	poll-tax
sculptor lapidum	mason
scyphus	cup
se	him
seculum	worldly affairs
sepiens	hay-maker
Septuagesima	Septuagesima Sunday
sepultura	buried
sericum	silk
servitor & serviens	servant
sestertius	shilling
silvacedus	woodcutter
simplex	of low rank
sobrina/us	cousin on mother's side
socius	fellow
solemnia nuptiarum	to celebrate a marriage
solidum	undivided property
solidus	shilling
soror	sister
sororius	sister's husband
spera	sideboard
spondea rotans	trundle bed
sponsalia	banns of marriage
sponsus/a	spouse

statim	at once
stuprata	pregnant out of wedlock
sudarium	napkin
suarium	shroud
sus	swine
sutor caligarius	hosier
sutor chirothecarius	glover
sutor vestarius	tailor
suus	own
taberna	tavern, inn
tabernio	inn-keeper
tabula	board, shutter
tabula mansalis	table
tallia	tally
tannator	tanner
tantellus	cousin
tector	thatcher
tenementum	house
testamentum	will, bequest
textator	weaver
tia	maternal aunt
traditio & tradux	inheritance
transfiguratio Domini	Transfiguration (August 6)
tumba	tomb
tunica	coat
ulna	ell (measure of length)
ulterior	additional
unicus/a	unmarried man/woman
uxor	Mrs., wife
vedovus	widower
viciatus	bastard
vidua	widow
vincula Sancti Petri	Saint Peter's Chains (Aug. 1)
warda	guardianship
xped	christened

INDEX